THE
WILL
OF A
NATION

THE WILL OF A NATION

AWAKENING THE CANADIAN SPIRIT

GEORGE RADWANSKI
and
JULIA LUTTRELL

Stoddart

First published in 1992 by
Stoddart Publishing Co. Limited
34 Lesmill Road
Toronto, Canada
M3B 2T6

CANADIAN CATALOGUING IN PUBLICATION DATA

Radwanski, George, 1947-
    The will of a nation: awakening the Canadian spirit

ISBN 0-7737-2637-3

1. Canada — Politics and government — 1980-
2. Nationalism — Canada. I. Luttrell, Julia.
II. Title.

FC630.R23'1992   320.971   C92-093967-8
F1034.2.R23 1992

Printed and bound in the United States of America

The publisher gratefully acknowledges the support of Canada Council,
Ontario Arts Council and Ontario Publishing Centre in the development of
writing and publishing in Canada.

For Adam, the finest son any father could want.
G.R.

For my son Jason, the love of my life.
J.L.

Contents

Author's Note

Every nation comes, sooner or later, to a defining moment in its history — a time when its people must decide whether they truly have the will and the faith to triumph together over adversity and go on to greater strengths as a society, or whether they will allow themselves to be torn apart. For many countries, that moment arrives dramatically amid war, revolution or civil strife. For Canada, the great test of our national spirit has crept up quietly, almost imperceptibly, but today it is none the less real. This book is an attempt to help understand why we are now in this situation, and how we can emerge from it strengthened rather than shattered.

Because so many of the judgments and ideas in this book are the product not of short-term research but of years of experience in a variety of capacities, the people who have contributed in one way or another are far too numerous to mention individually. They know who they are, and they know they are appreciated.

In the actual preparation of the book, however, Bob Kisin, Naomi Levy, Michael Coughlin and Carolyn Galea very kindly agreed to serve as an ad hoc "focus group" that met several times to give us their perspectives and provide a sounding-board for our ideas. As well, Michael Coughlin read the manuscript and made valuable suggestions, for which we are most grateful.

Jack Stoddart, Donald G. Bastian, Angel Guerra and their colleagues at Stoddart Publishing have been a pleasure to work with.

This book has turned out to be the product of a collaboration as gratifying as it was unanticipated. My friend Julia Luttrell set out to help me with the research for this project. But her qualities of intellect and insight are such that her contribution began from the outset to far surpass the research function. Through many months of discussion, she helped to frame and focus the thoughts to be presented, contributing important ideas and perceptions of her own. Then she agreed to work alongside me throughout the writing process, helping to find the right words to make complex subject matter come alive. I believe the result owes much to the blending of our similar philosophies but very different vantage points — hers being one that exemplifies the best Canadian qualities of will and determination, qualities that enabled her to bring herself largely through self-education from a childhood in Northern Ontario with very limited opportunities to being one of the most creative and intellectually vibrant people I know. Because this became "our book" in a way that could not adequately be reflected in a mere acknowledgement, I asked Julia Luttrell to share the credit — or blame — as co-author. I am proud to have worked with her, and deeply appreciative of her contribution.

George Radwanski
Toronto

ONE

From Confidence
to Chaos

A S RECENTLY AS THE SPRING OF 1984, Canada was a country with a brilliant future.

We knew who we were, even if we were reluctant to extol our virtues. We had a quiet, but profound, sense of being one of the most fortunate nations in the world. We prided ourselves on being free, prosperous, relatively tolerant, and non-violent. We took satisfaction in being respected in the world as peacekeepers, leaders in environmental responsibility, and a voice for good. And perhaps above all, we were glad to be a society that took care of its people.

We felt, for the most part, united as a nation. Our new Constitution, highlighted by the Charter of Rights and Freedoms, was more a source of pride than of division. The people of Quebec, having voted no to separatism, had turned their attention to building a prosperous, outward-looking economy; debates about language, culture and new powers for the Quebec government no longer dominated the agenda.

We had our share of problems — unemployment, poverty and regional disaffection among them — but few doubted they were manageable. People expected the economy to bounce back, as it had in the past. New initiatives would be developed over time to address the still-too-high poverty rate, because that was the Canadian way. Regional grievances were part of the normal tensions and give-and-take in a federal state, and they would be addressed as such on an ongoing basis. But the commitment to Canada remained strong.

What kept all the problems in perspective and provided the bedrock of Canadian unity and confidence was a sense that our destiny was ours to control. Canada was still a young nation — still building, still growing — and everything was possible.

Now, less than a decade later, Canada has been shaken to the very wellsprings of our existence as a nation. The optimism that sustained us until so recently, today seems very long ago and far away. We suddenly feel as if our best years may be in the past.

Instead of coping with the normal ups and downs of the economy, we find ourselves seeing something alarmingly close to economic collapse. In place of the habitual regional grumblings, there is a barely muted fury in every part of the land; everywhere there is a search for scapegoats, and protest parties are proliferating. Where so recently we prided ourselves on our independence, we now feel increasingly that control over our destiny has been handed to the United States. Where in the past we would periodically grow disenchanted with a political party and vote for change, today we feel mistrustful of all politicians and under attack by government itself.

Our emerging national confidence and sense of identity have abruptly evaporated; suddenly, countless studies and commissions are taking the national pulse. Yet instead of achieving clarity, we are approaching despair. People are wearying to the point of scarcely caring anymore. For the first time in our history, the break-up of Canada is being calmly, almost dispassionately, discussed as a real possibility. Astonishing numbers of people are asking themselves what's so special about Canada; is it really worth struggling to preserve?

Experts are debating whether the separation of Quebec is more likely to be amicable or bitter, how the national debt should be apportioned in the event of break-up, whether we need a corridor between Ontario and Atlantic Canada. There is talk about whether remaining provinces would be better off banding together or drifting into union with the United States. What a few years ago would have been dismissed as absurd, morbid fantasizing is now accepted matter-of-factly.

We are like a family that one day enjoys a perfectly normal dinner and evening together and the next morning is packing its bags and arguing over who will get the silverware as everyone suddenly prepares to head off forever in different directions.

The absurd thing is that there is no reason for it — nothing irreversible has yet happened. All the important reasons why Canada commanded our confidence and our hopes until a few short years ago, all the reasons we have been such a viable, vibrant and promising country, are still in place today, or still salvageable.

What we are experiencing is a profound crisis of the will.

How did we come to this? How have we gone so quickly from confidence and normalcy to a kind of collective nervous breakdown, a rapidly accelerating collapse of our national spirit?

The reality is that a society, like an individual, can
be a surprisingly fragile emotional entity when subjected to too many shocks and strains over a concen-
trated period, and that is what has happened to
Canada. Our self-image, our sense of our key values,
and our understanding of who we are as a nation have
all come under relentless, sustained attack — not from
some foreign power or some series of natural disasters,
but from our own national government. For the first
time in our history, we have a government that is
intent not on building, but on tearing down. Every
previous government that was in power for a prolonged
period added something to our national fabric; for the
first time, with the Progressive Conservatives under
Prime Minister Brian Mulroney, we have been experiencing a government that systematically does nothing
but rend that fabric.

All the things we took for granted about Canada have
been disappearing before our eyes. In a nation where
some 435,000 manufacturing jobs have disappeared in
just two years, prosperity seems an irretrievable dream.
Where until so recently we prided ourselves on being a
caring society, we see the social safety net unravelling at
every seam. Unemployment insurance has been cut
back, funding for welfare has been slashed, we see the
homeless in our streets. Food banks — the soup lines of
the 1990s — are proliferating. And now even medicare
is threatened. Taxes keep rising, and we are getting less
and less back for our money.

National institutions that were symbolic of our identity
are being dismantled at every turn. Our railways, our air
transportation network, the CBC, the Canada Council,
Petro-Canada and other key elements of the Canadian

foundation that were built up over decades have all come under relentless attack.

In short, for the first time in our history we have a government that is actively working at dismantling virtually all the key elements of Canada as we know it: our transportation links, our communications and cultural links, our social support links, the underpinnings of our economy, and our independence. Worst of all, we have a government that is working, through all this, at dismantling our sense of who we are as a nation.

National values that have shaped our development throughout history are scorned by the national government itself. We are told we can no longer afford compassion; there is room only for "competitiveness." We are urged to believe it is no longer right for the national government to ensure fairness and sharing from coast to coast; everyone is to be at the mercy of "market forces." We are required to accept the belief that building our future is an out-of-reach luxury; all we can afford is to whittle down the achievements of the past.

No wonder Canadians are confused and despairing.

A nation, like an individual, can thrive only in the presence of ongoing hopes, dreams and goals. Especially for a young country like Canada, the abrupt withdrawal of hope can only be lethal. The evolution of our Canadian values, indeed the whole character of our society, has been shaped by the great task of overcoming challenge after challenge and building a nation together. Throughout our history, the powerful if often unspoken sense of shared goals and undertakings was a bond that unified us. The wrenching away of our capacity to hope and dream together, to join in building a better future for our children, could only leave us profoundly divided.

Such has been the legacy of the Mulroney government. Only by recognizing and understanding what has happened, how we got here and what is being taken away from us can we set ourselves on a different course and save our nation.

What's So Special About Canada?

What is so compellingly attractive about Canada? ...
We do not have a very good track record.
Our products have not been of the highest quality.
Our deliveries have been lacking in reliability.
Our expertise has been in large measure borrowed.
Our technology has been purchased.
What the hell makes us so special?

PRIME MINISTER BRIAN MULRONEY,

FORTUNE MAGAZINE INTERVIEW, MARCH 1985

I N ONLY A CENTURY and a quarter since Confederation, Canadians have shaped out of the North American wilderness one of the most privileged societies on the face of the earth. Ranking among the seven most prosperous nations in the world, Canada is rich not only in the abundance of our resources and the magnificence of our land, but also in the diversity and the character of our people. We have long been known as one of the most tolerant, progressive, innovative, caring and peaceful societies in existence.

Our accomplishments have not been mere accidents of history. They are the result of conscious choices made by

Canadians at every stage of the nation's development. The Canada we have known was literally willed into being.

From its very beginning, Canada was an act of the will. Logically speaking, it made no sense to try to turn a few settlements north of the 49th parallel into a full-fledged nation. We had to prevail against the great distances and rugged terrain between our Atlantic and Pacific coasts, the punishing rigours of our northern climate, the challenges of reconciling two founding languages and cultures, the sparsity of our population and the presence of a far larger neighbour to our south.

If our predecessors had simply left events to run their course, if they had left everything up to "free enterprise" or "market forces," there would never have been a Canada. Instead, they recognized that all these obstacles could be overcome only by a constant act of collective will, a fierce determination to act together — together as individuals, and together through government acting on our behalf. Thus, we became one of the most envied countries in the world by evolving a uniquely Canadian approach to nation-building: an exceptionally strong sense of community combined with a high degree of government involvement.

From the beginning, the national government was seen as an instrument of our collective will. The Fathers of Confederation understood that English and French, Protestants and Catholics, East and West could be kept together as a single country only by a central government strong enough to guarantee minority rights and regional rights and to serve as the leading force for unity. In contrast to the United States, where emphasis on states' rights had by then led to a bloody civil war, virtually all the areas of jurisdiction considered crucial in those days were entrusted to our federal government.

Also from the beginning, we opted not only for a strong national government, but for an activist one as well. Canadians have always recognized that there are some things we all have to do together through our government, through public ownership or public intervention, because market forces alone can't or won't make them happen. That was the Canadian way in the days of John A. Macdonald's National Policy — high tariffs to protect newborn Canadian industries from foreign competition, and railway-building and large-scale immigration to open up the West. It was still the Canadian way a century later, with Pierre Trudeau's creation of such national instruments as the Foreign Investment Review Agency and Petro-Canada.

We would not have a Canada as we know it if successive federal governments — Conservative as well as Liberal — had not acted directly to meet vital national needs. We could not have thrived without a national railway system, and later a national airline, to span our great distances and bind the country together. Our governments ensured their creation, and they became Crown corporations owned by us all. We needed a national broadcasting system to reflect our own culture and identity amid a flood of cultural imports and to allow Canadians in every region to communicate with one another. Our national government created the CBC, publicly owned as well.

The same was true of our great social programs. The Canadian sense of community probably was shaped from earliest days by the challenges of living in isolated settlements amid the rigours of our climate and terrain. People recognized their interdependence and pitched in to help one another, especially in times of hardship and emergency. That same spirit was in evidence in the 1920s, when Prairie farmers banded together in cooperatives, or wheat pools, to store and market their crops. Later, as our society became ever more complex, pressure grew for our sense of community to be expressed in more comprehensive, structured ways.

Here, too, we chose to make government the instrument of our collective will. Step by step we built up our social support network, beginning with old-age pensions in 1927 and culminating in the creation of national medicare in 1966. It became the expression of a deep-rooted Canadian will that no Canadian should be abandoned to suffer unassisted the ravages of sickness, unemployment, poverty or old age.

It is true that our safety net evolved gradually, amid a great many political battles, rather than being part of any single master plan placed before the Canadian public. Like so much about Canada, the changes were incremental rather than radical. As all the elements took shape, the system as a whole found a place not only in the lives but also in the hearts of Canadians.

Our social support system, through the profoundly decent values it represents, has come to reflect the very best purposes of human societies in a way that relatively few other countries have been able to attain. It is who we are and what Canada is all about.

From earliest days of civilization, humans have grouped together — in families, tribes, villages, cities and nations — out of recognition that interdependence and cooperation promise a better existence than life in isolation. The greatest promise lies not merely in the advantages of hunting, farming or manufacturing together, but in the security of knowing that in times of personal adversity there will be a source of help. Most small, simple social units take care of their own when they become sick, impoverished or old. In many large, modern societies, however, that is not always sufficiently the case.

The fact that in this country we do so — not always nearly well enough, but better than most — is a key aspect of what makes Canada special. It has become a defining part of our national character, this recognition that not only decency but also enlightened self-interest require us to try to ensure a certain basic quality of life for all our fellow citizens.

The most obvious self-interest is that few among us can be absolutely sure that we or our children will never fall prey to serious illness, unemployment or a financially uncertain old age. The safety net protects us all, not just abstract others. But beyond that, our social support network reflects at least an intuitive understanding that no society can truly thrive if there is misery in its midst, if people are hungry in the midst of plenty, if the sick face not only physical but also financial torment, if children's futures are short-changed by their parents' poverty. In such a society, resentment runs rampant, criminality increases, guilt afflicts the sensitive, a general meanness of spirit threatens to take hold among the rest, consensus is elusive and the quality of *everyone's* life is ultimately diminished.

It would be difficult to feel very proud of such a society; Canada's ability to inspire quiet pride through a very different approach has been one of our great unifying strengths as a nation. Our social programs for individuals are, of course, only one aspect of what makes Canada special. Our national will to use the federal government as an active instrument of unity and fairness has also been reflected in the way we treat our regions. The disparities in affluence among our provinces and regions are still regrettably large, but if everything had been left to market forces alone, they would be enormous. The standard of living of Canadians in some regions would have virtually nothing in common with the standard of those living in other parts of the country.

Instead, we have evolved the principle of equalization, under which the federal government redistributes some of the revenues it collects from the richer provinces to the less affluent ones. These transfer payments have enabled the governments of the poorer provinces to provide their publics with a level of services that would otherwise have been unattainable. Thus, through our national government, we have chosen to help ensure that all Canadians, wherever they live, are able to enjoy at least a certain common minimum quality of life. At the same time, federal expenditures on regional development in those provinces have been aimed at building up local economies, to provide greater equality of employment opportunity across the country.

This approach sets us apart from a great many other countries, which allow regional disparities to be addressed primarily through population movements away from depressed areas to more prosperous ones. We have said, instead, that a Canadian in New Brunswick or Saskatchewan who wants good education and health care for his or her children, and a decent livelihood, shouldn't have to move to Montreal, Toronto or Vancouver. The approach we have evolved recognizes that you cannot build a strong and united nation by depopulating its regions, breaking people's attachment to their particular piece of our land, and encouraging everyone to go where the prosperity already is. We have opted, rather, to work to bring a fair share of Canada's prosperity to every part of the country.

This commitment to sharing — sharing among individuals, and sharing among regions — is a common thread that runs through the evolution of Canadian policies. It is a key element of what makes Canada special. We are a nation that has chosen, through its government, not to opt for a social Darwinism that leaves people or entire parts of the country to the mercy of survival of the fittest. Rather, we have evolved an approach that is closer to the model of a family or a closely knit community that takes care of its own and strives to share its bounty and its burdens as equitably as possible.

It would be wrong to overly romanticize this. We are far from being some blissful Shangri-la or Camelot where everyone has lived in perfect harmony and partnership. Canadians never sat down at some dramatic moment and together said: "Let's all share with one another." Nevertheless, that commitment to sharing is a choice we have collectively made, time after time, through our choices of governments and our choices of the policies we supported. It has been one of our most distinguishing characteristics.

Other key aspects of what makes Canada special also revolve around values that have come to characterize our behaviour as a nation. For example, when people in other countries describe their perception of Canada, one of the words most frequently used is "tolerant."

We may not always perceive ourselves that way. Certainly it is easy enough to point to moments of intolerance: anti-English behaviour in Quebec, anti-French backlashes in other provinces, incidents of racism against members of visible minorities. Yet the fact is, these are *incidents*, deviations from the norm. What is not an incident but an historical pattern has been the treatment of our aboriginal people; Canadians are finally coming to recognize it as a national shame that must be rectified. Still, Canada, though far from perfect, is one of the most tolerant nations on earth.

People come here from every part of the world, from countries at war with each other, and live side by side as neighbours, knowing we will not stand for having foreign conflicts imported onto Canadian soil. And yet we do not expect them to give up their identities to live here. The Canadian way has been not only to tolerate but to encourage cultural diversity, recognizing that people need not surrender their pride in their ethnic origins to participate fully in Canadian life.

We are a society that has been spared the intolerance built into rigid class systems. We have a Charter of Rights and Freedoms that prohibits virtually every form of unfair discrimination. Historically we have been tolerant in our approach to resolving conflicts. It may be a cliché to say that Canadians prefer compromise to confrontation — yet that is a preference which over the years has enabled us to evolve as a remarkably peaceful and civil society, for the most part avoiding the violence, profound rifts and irreconcilable bitterness that have marred the history of so many countries.

Perhaps it is an offshoot of this tolerance, this mistrustfulness of extremes, that makes us tend to be so diffident about our sense of national identity. We Canadians are always reluctant to speak of Canada, out loud, in terms of being superior or exceptional, even though there are many respects in which our country is both.

We even tend to be embarrassed, as Canadians, about the extent to which we define ourselves in terms of how we differ from the United States. It has become conventional wisdom to regard this sort of self-definition as somehow negative, because it focuses on what we are not, rather than on what we are. Yet such definition is not only natural but essential for a country living in the shadow of a neighbouring giant ten times its size — a giant, moreover, with the same language and at least superficial similarities of culture. So great is the sheer magnetic force of an economy and population ten times our size, coupled with the active U.S. effort to export its culture worldwide, that the only way Canada can survive independently is by a constant positive act of the will: we continually have to *choose* to be Canada, independent and distinct, or we will cease to be. And the only way to sustain that will is to understand, and to frequently recall, the differences that justify the effort it takes to remain apart from the United States.

Beneath the superficial similarities, the differences between our respective values and cultures are fundamental. At root, the United States is a vastly more individualistic society than Canada. From their earliest days, Americans have prized a spirit of "every man for himself," while Canadians have preferred a spirit of helping one another. Where the mythic image of the U.S. frontier is the lone gunfighter riding off into the sunset, our corresponding image of Western settlement is the barn-raising — neighbours all pitching in to help new settlers build their barn in a day. We Canadians value individual rights, but we temper them far more with a sense of collective responsibility.

This difference between countries is reflected in the stated national purposes set out in our respective constitutions. The highest goals for the United States are "life, liberty and the pursuit of happiness" — all objectives that focus on the individual. Our goals, by contrast, are "peace, order and good government" — all objectives that focus on how we relate to one another.

These are not abstract, theoretical differences. They pervade nearly every aspect of our respective daily lives. Unlike in the United States, for instance, in Canada no one could get elected by campaigning on the right to bear arms.

We Canadians believe that the individual's right to bear arms is superseded by the collective right of the rest of us not to get shot by someone bearing arms. We Canadians believe that real individual freedom is more than just the absence of constraint or oppression by the state. We recognize, through the evolution of the policies we have demanded and supported, that real freedom is the freedom to live dignified and fulfilling lives.

No one is meaningfully free if he or she is hungry and homeless, or if grinding poverty requires spending every waking moment trying to figure out how to feed, clothe and shelter one's children. A sick person is not free if lack of money cuts off access to first-rate health care to cure a debilitating illness or prevent a premature death. A child is not free if inadequate, underfunded education systems deny him or her the knowledge and skills needed to participate successfully in a knowledge-intensive world. The elderly are not free if insufficient income or inadequate care and support facilities leave them unable to do more than wait out their remaining time in squalor or lonely isolation.

Our differing values are reflected in aspects of the quality of everyday life in Canada and the United States.

If you are brought to the emergency room of a Canadian hospital, nobody checks your credit rating before checking your pulse. Unlike in parts of the U.S. Sun Belt where unionization has not been allowed to take hold, we do not have citizens working for near-starvation wages without insurance or other benefits. Because we have not accepted the extremes of poverty and the socio-economic ghettos that are taken for granted in large U.S. cities, our crime rates are vastly lower — and all of us are the safer for it.

We Canadians are not being "anti-American" when we note such differences and resolve to stay on our own course. Indeed, it is probably fair to say that most Canadians like Americans; it is the United States we are wary of. The values that shape life in that country have historically been alien to us. If they are satisfactory to Americans, that is no concern of ours. But we have never wanted those values to become our own, and with good cause. Our strongest defence against that happening has always been a combination of noting American vices and recognizing our own virtues. Both elements of that combination have begun to slip in recent years, under the aegis of a prime minister who asks, "What's so special about Canada?"

Rediscovering our national will requires us first to answer that question clearly and unequivocally in our minds and hearts: There is much that is special about Canada — so very much.

We are a society dedicated to the profoundly human values of sharing, tolerance and a sense of shared responsibility for one another. We are a peaceful, civil society. We are a young nation, among the youngest in the world, unshackled by history. We are not captives of bad habits acquired over centuries. We do not bear the scars of revolution, civil war or racial or ethnic hatreds. Our vast and beautiful land is among the most resource-rich in the world; we have everything in abundance — oil, minerals, water, wood, fertile farmland, ocean fisheries. We are respected abroad as a country that has been a voice for fairness and peace. We have never been an international colonial power; we have never subjugated other countries to our will. We are an Atlantic nation, and a Pacific one. As an industrialized nation that is also a developing one, we have the unique capacity to serve as a bridge between the developed countries and the Third World.

And perhaps most important, we are a nation that is still being built. We can do anything we want. Nothing constrains us — not history, not geography, not lack of resources, not lack of freedom. Our future is still ours to shape in whatever way we choose.

For Canada, perhaps more than for any other nation in the world today, nothing is impossible.

THREE

A Caricature
of Competitiveness

NATIONAL POLITICS IN CANADA has never swung widely between extremes of left and right. Rather, the Canadian way has historically been a remarkably consistent straight line, situated moderately left of centre.

Canadians have consistently wanted, and have voted for, governments that were progressive, people-oriented in the sense of emphasizing both sufficient employment and a strong social safety net, interventionist when necessary to protect the general public interest or the most vulnerable, and at least mildly nationalistic — in short, governments that focused on national development and held out the hope of an ever better future.

All three major federal parties — the Liberals, the Progressive Conservatives and the New Democratic Party — were arrayed along that same straight line, with differences only of degree. There was never a radical polarization in our national politics.

Whenever Canadians voted for a change of government, it wasn't because we wanted a radical shift of direction. We were comfortable having all three parties grouped in a fairly narrow mainstream. When we voted for change, it was because the government of the day was perceived to have strayed too far off the line, to have become too far removed from ordinary people and their concerns.

For most of the past half-century, the federal Liberals were perceived as the most adept at adhering to this consistent "Canadian line" of government. When they were seen to have drifted too far out of touch under Louis St. Laurent in 1957, voters turned to the Tories under John Diefenbaker, with his populism and "Northern vision." When Diefenbaker in time proved unable to live up to his promise and his government fell apart, power reverted to the Liberals, first under Lester Pearson and then under Pierre Trudeau. And when in 1979 the Trudeau administration seemed lethargic and drifting after more than a decade in power, people put their trust briefly in the Tories under Joe Clark.

Each time, the voters simply shifted their support to whichever party then offered the best promise of delivering those same things they wanted all along.

That's all people thought they were doing, yet again, in the 1984 general election. After a decade and a half of Liberal government, there was an underlying feeling among the public that it was time to give a chance to a fresh team. Even more important, the new Tory leader, Brian Mulroney, succeeded in presenting himself as a more authentic political heir to Trudeau than did the new Liberal leader, John Turner.

Turner, with his strained look, nervous mannerisms and wildly flashing eyes, made people uncomfortable. He seemed an oddly remote and unapproachable Establishment figure, awkwardly transplanted from Toronto's Bay Street. It was Mulroney who successfully presented himself as an earnest, straightforward man of the people, who seemed closer to the progressive "Canadian line" of policy. The Tory leader did talk vaguely about making government leaner, more efficient and less involved in things it didn't need to be doing — what Canadian could disagree with that? — but his core message focused on the traditional Canadian agenda. While Turner harrumphed about the size of the federal deficit and hinted that government programs might have to be slashed, it was Mulroney who told Canadians that his absolute priority would be "jobs, jobs, jobs" and pledged that maintaining our social programs intact would be "a sacred trust." Mulroney also vowed not to increase personal taxes for ordinary Canadians, but to institute a minimum income tax for the rich to keep them from abusing tax loopholes.

When Canadians gave Brian Mulroney and the Progressive Conservatives a huge majority on September 4, 1984, they therefore had every right to believe they were simply electing yet another mainstream government that would carry forward the values on which the strength of our nation has been built.

Less than two months after the election, there was the first startling sign that something was dramatically wrong — that Canadians had somehow elected a government far outside the mainstream occupied by all its predecessors. As one of its very first major acts, the new Conservative government tabled in Parliament an economic blueprint document entitled "A New Direction for Canada: An Agenda for Economic Renewal." That document made it clear, in the bluntest terms, that Canada was now in the hands of something entirely unforeseen in the preceding election campaign and

never before experienced in our national politics: a doctrinaire right-wing federal government.

Having scarcely mentioned it during the entire election
campaign, Mulroney and his Tories suddenly declared the
federal deficit to be an overwhelming national crisis. In
the name of reducing that deficit, their overriding priority
would be the sharp cutting back of the role and activities
of the federal government. Social programs, energy programs, regional development, agricultural support measures, Via Rail subsidies, foreign aid — all these and more
were to be hacked relentlessly, for our own good.

Like a scene in one of those sci-fi movies where a seemingly helpful character suddenly peels off his artificial face
and turns out to be a razor-fanged horror, the new Mulroney
government sprang on us the news that it had come into
our national life to slash everything in sight. And, perhaps
most horrifying of all, it coolly told us that this was what we
wanted. "On September 4, Canadians voted for change,"
the blueprint document stated. "The mandate of
September 4 reflects as well a sombre judgment about
Canada's poor economic performance in the recent past."

Having never been told that the Tories intended to
take this right-wing approach, let alone given them a
mandate for it, Canadians were understandably confused. If the outpouring of public outrage wasn't greater
at that moment, it may have been because this outright
distortion of the truth by our own national government
— being told there was a right-wing mandate, when it
had never been given — was still then a new experience
for Canadians. We had been accustomed, on the whole,
to being able to trust our government.

It would have been easy enough for any individual
voter to think perhaps he or she had missed the point of

the election: "I know I wasn't voting for this kind of stuff, but maybe everybody else was. Maybe I just wasn't paying close enough attention to what was being said. Otherwise, how could the government say now that it has this mandate?"

But by spring, after a Tory budget that snipped away at the "sacred trust" by reducing the indexation of old-age pensions, senior citizen Solange Denis was crystallising the feelings of a great many Canadians when she shouted at Mulroney on Parliament Hill: "You lied to us. You got us to vote for you and then it's good-bye, Charlie Brown!"

Yet the Mulroney government succeeded in further confusing Canadians even as it disillusioned them ever more deeply. Had Mulroney and his ministers talked candidly about their ideology on its own merits, the public almost certainly would have rejected them as hopelessly out of sync with the nation's wants and needs and turfed them out after one term. But by cloaking their agenda in unrelenting emphasis on the deficit and Canadian economic competitiveness, the Tories constantly hammered home the message that we had *no choice* but to follow their approach; any other course, they insisted, would spell disaster. Thus the Tories succeeded in beginning to erode confidence in the values and policies that had served us so well. People didn't like what was happening, but they were being told by their own government that there was no choice, that we could no longer afford Canada as we had known it.

In reality, the agenda pursued by the Tories since 1984 has not been a crisis response to special and threatening Canadian circumstances. It has been an ideological agenda patterned on Reaganism in the United States and Thatcherism in Britain, an ideology as unrelated to

Canadian needs as it is to Conservative thought in Canada throughout our history. The ideology adopted by Mulroney and his team is not genuine contemporary conservatism but "free enterprise-ism," a kind of extreme laissez-faire belief that the best government in all circumstances is the least government. Under this doctrine, spending money on government programs "crowds out" spending by business, government intervention of any kind drives away investment, and social programs discourage individual initiative while making us uncompetitive because of their costs. Government is seen, by definition, as an enemy, an oppressor. Hence, whenever some aspect of government involvement is cut, power is being turned back "to the people" and only good things can result.

It doesn't work that way in reality. When the national government vacates some sphere of authority or activity, the resulting power vacuum is not filled by ordinary people for the common good. It is filled by other powerful interests — big business or other levels of government — pursuing their own advantages. When air transportation is deregulated, ordinary Canadians don't get to decide which routes will be maintained. The decision-making power reverts to the airlines, which keep the profitable, heavily travelled routes and chop the rest — even if the more lightly travelled routes are essential to the survival or development of communities or regions. When the government ceases to require that foreign investment or takeovers provide increased employment and research opportunities for Canadians, ordinary citizens cannot do so in its stead. The means to protect the common good is not transferred; it is surrendered. When the national government withdraws from funding health care, ordinary people do not become more powerful —

or healthier. They must either pay higher provincial taxes to make up the shortfall, see their health care cut back, or both.

It is scarcely surprising, therefore, that the driving force behind this ideology comes not from broadly based public opinion, but from the business community and particularly from big business. When government stops regulating an activity, companies are free to make their own choices, based solely on the profit motive. When the government privatizes a Crown corporation, other companies need no longer have their behaviour compared with that of an entity which must take the public interest into account. When social programs are dismantled, people will eventually be desperate enough to work for much lower wages, increasing corporate profits but undermining the Canadian quality of life. When spheres of jurisdiction are transferred from a single national government to ten provincial ones, businesses will have a better chance to play off province against province in search of the conditions they want in areas such as environmental standards or worker protection.

There is nothing "anti-business" about recognizing why the business sector actively seeks the absolute minimum of government involvement. Corporations seek above all to maximize their profits; they see that as their role, with other considerations lagging far behind. They may be short-sighted even in terms of their own best interests, but they are certainly within their rights in vigorously advocating what they believe will serve them best.

The problem arises when a government takes that advocacy as its own, instead of meeting its responsibility to uphold the broad public interest by drawing a fair balance between pressures from the whole range of competing interests. What the Mulroney government has done is adopt the agenda of one powerful interest group — big business — as its own, and that is deeply, deeply wrong.

A democratic society exists for one purpose only: the well-being of *all* the people who are its members. The role of government in such a society is not to succumb to the most powerful or to ally itself with them, but to serve as the instrument of ordinary people in ensuring fairness, protecting the most vulnerable, promoting sustainable growth and ensuring that the most powerful — whether individuals, corporations or organized labour — are *not* left to trample roughshod over the rest.

In a young and growing country like Canada, our government must go even further. It must lead, on our behalf, in creating an environment where people can be secure enough about the basics of life to be able to realize their full potential, where we can focus as a society on innovation, creativity and constant development in new and ever more progressive directions.

That is where the Mulroney government's ideological doctrine of unfettered reliance on free enterprise or "market forces" — in other words, on the profit motive — falls apart. Market forces, by their very nature, care only whether there is a dollar to be made; they are indifferent to human consequences. Market forces are incapable of caring about the human toll when people are thrown out of work or are paid too little to lead a dignified existence. Market forces are incapable of caring about the environment, about poverty, about national unity, about the protection of Canadian independence, about strengthening the values and characteristics that make Canada distinct and special. They are by nature indifferent to our quality of life.

That is why we Canadians have historically chosen to have not an unrestrictedly free-market economy but a "mixed" economy — that is, an economy that recognizes the importance of market forces but, where necessary, channels and counterbalances those forces with government involvement to ensure that human and national interest considerations come first.

To veer from that approach, as the Mulroney government has done, is to lose sight that our people do not exist to serve the economy; the economy exists to serve people. Actual impact on people — not abstract considerations like free enterprise, competitiveness or globalization — is the test that must be applied to determine whether policies work or make sense.

Yes, it is essential for Canada to be internationally competitive. But competitive for what purpose? If we were, for instance, to achieve competitiveness by putting half our labour force out of work and paying the rest the kind of starvation wages earned in Third World countries, would that be a success? Who would benefit?

Neither the Conservatives nor their backers in the business community have said honestly to Canadians what exactly it would take, in real life, to be competitive in the sense they are advocating. They justify all sorts of Draconian measures as necessary steps on the road to competitiveness, but no one wants to talk about what the destination would look like if we ever reached it.

It's not only the Americans who are our international competitors. Canadian industries encounter even tougher competition, both at home and in the international marketplace, from Taiwan, Korea, Mexico — from a whole range of countries with very different social structures and far lower wage levels and standards of living. To

compete with them in the mass production of industrialized goods, we would have to lower our standard of living to match theirs. Yet the mantra of competitiveness is
simply an endless chant that we have to tighten our
belts, that we must become more productive. No one
has told Canadians *at what point* the kind of competitiveness the Tories advocate would be achieved. How
far, precisely, would we have to streamline? How many
people have to lose their jobs for the desired level of
productivity to be achieved? How many pay cuts do we
have to take before we become "competitive"?

If the Mulroney government or the business community were to answer such bottom-line questions
forthrightly — to say, for instance, that average industrial
earnings would have to be $200 a week instead of $528,
or unemployment would have to reach 25 per cent to
achieve the necessary belt-tightening — there could at
least be an honest debate. We could ask ourselves: "Are
we willing to do that? Is that kind of competitiveness
worth pursuing? What would we gain from it?"

It does not suffice to say that if our corporations are
competitive and therefore profitable, ordinary people
automatically benefit through some sort of trickle-down
effect. Those profits are primarily paid out in dividends
to comparatively affluent shareholders, whether individuals or institutions, many of them located outside
Canada because of the heavy foreign ownership in our
economy. Only a comparatively small proportion of corporate profits is paid in Canadian taxes to be used for
the general public benefit.

So competitiveness and profitability are not goods in
themselves, in isolation from how they are achieved. It
makes no sense for Canadians to pursue a strategy that puts

us into competition with people with whom we cannot possibly compete without cutting our own throats. We need to focus instead on developing our capacity to compete in areas of our own strength, where we have potential advantages and can generate genuine wealth. Yes, the world is changing and we must change with it. But the only change worth pursuing is change for the better, change consistent with the kind of Canada we want to have.

The only competitiveness that can truly benefit our society is a competitiveness that provides decently paid jobs or other meaningful social roles for all Canadians, and that safeguards and strengthens the social support network that is such an important element in ensuring an adequate quality of life for all Canadians. Yet that is precisely what the Conservatives are prepared to sacrifice on the altar of a Reaganite, Thatcherite caricature of "competitiveness."

In pursuit of this new Tory agenda so alien to our national character, our values and our history, the Mulroney government has already exacted a terrible price from Canadians in virtually every area of our lives. We have been hit hard in our pursuit of social justice, in the foundations and fabric of our society, in the workings of our economy, in our freedom to chart our own course as a sovereign nation and even in our dedication to remaining together as a nation at all.

Slashing the Safety Net

I N LESS THAN A DECADE the Mulroney government has managed to fray virtually every strand of the social safety net that Canadians so painstakingly wove over decades. Not a single important area of social policy has escaped the knife of the prime minister who had pledged that social programs would be a "sacred trust." Unemployment insurance, welfare payments, old-age pensions, family allowances, public housing, the progressiveness of the tax system and even medicare have all been attacked and weakened.

In doing this, the Tories have not only undermined an important element of our sense of who we are as a nation, and made us a much less fair society. They have also, paradoxically, undermined the very capacity for genuine economic competitiveness they claim to want so badly. They, and their backers in the business community, have failed utterly to understand that in a country like today's Canada, strong social programs are not only fair. They are also sensible economics.

Canada, like every other advanced industrialized society including the United States, is in the midst of a socio-economic transformation every bit as fundamental as the earlier shift from agrarian to industrial societies. This transformation can roughly be described as a shift in the preponderance of economic activity from the production of goods to the provision of services.

More than 75 per cent of Canadians are now employed in the service sector, which comprises all forms of activity other than mining, forestry, farming, fishing and manufacturing. The service sector now also accounts for more than 72 per cent of Canada's gross domestic product. This emergence of the service sector as by far the largest component of our economy does not mean that manufacturing is no longer important, any more than the transition from agrarian to industrial society meant that farming no longer mattered. What it does mean is that with automation and other factors steadily reducing the share of the labour force required to produce all the goods we can use ourselves or export, the structure and the needs of our economy are quite different from what we used to take for granted. In the type of industrial economy we previously had, the most important inputs were capital and raw materials. Competitive advantage rested with those companies, and those societies, that had ready access to money to build plants and buy machinery, and to plentiful and cheap raw materials to transform in those plants.

In the emerging new economy, the most important inputs are people and knowledge. In virtually every service sector industry, as well as in sophisticated manufacturing, the key determinant of success or failure is the human factor: the skills, knowledge and performance of the people involved. An airline whose staff are skilled and efficient enough to adhere to schedules and to meet customer expectations is likely to fare better than one whose performance is unpredictable as a result of poor planning and sloppy work. A restaurant is unlikely to thrive if waiters are ill-informed, rude, slow and forgetful, or if the chef cooks badly. The quality of a bank, a hospital or an engineering firm depends mainly on the expertise, judgment and motivation of personnel. And in the manufacturing sector as well, the industries that have the best chance of surviving and being competitive are the sophisticated, specialized ones that require high-quality, well-educated and well-trained workers.

What the Tories and their mentors in the business community have failed to understand is that in such an economy where people are the most important asset, a strong network of social support measures is not a financial drain but a vital instrument of economic development.

It is vital, first of all, in easing the transitions that our economy — like economies around the world — is undergoing. As it becomes impractical to compete in some fields and we need to shift our energies to others, or as new technologies come into effect, many people have already been dislocated by change. Many others fear they yet may be affected. The only way to make the uncertainties of such rapid change less frightening and damaging is to ensure a strong sense that we are one another's co-insurers, and that no one will be left alone at the mercy of forces beyond his or her control. That is why a strong safety net of income maintenance and social support measures is absolutely essential if people are to accept the continuous industrial adjustment and labour force flexibility that our new economy requires. It would be absurd, after all, to expect workers to cooperate in the introduction of labour-displacing technologies, to learn new skills or to accept the prospect of periodic job changes, unless they can feel certain that society will repay that cooperation by meeting their basic needs if they become displaced. If that certainty is denied them and they resist change by every available means, as anyone in his or her right mind would do under those circumstances, the inevitable outcome will be escalating bitterness and labour-management confrontation. That, in turn, is bound to impede flexibility and adjustment and to hobble our economic performance to everyone's detriment.

But facilitating change is only one reason why supportive social policies make good business sense. Even more important, in a new economy whose key characteristic is reliance on human resources, it makes all the sense in the world to nurture those resources. Such nurturing requires not only first-rate education, but also ensuring excellent health care, child care, availability of care for elderly dependants, and the absence of excessive anxiety about the possibility of falling into need.

It stands to reason, for instance, that a healthy employee will be more effective than an ailing one, or that businesses will needlessly suffer disadvantages if key employees needing surgery or other treatment languish for prolonged periods on sick leave because underfunded hospitals have them on waiting lists. Likewise, workers distracted by worry about makeshift care arrangements for a young child or an elderly dependant are likely to be less effective than those who are confident that first-rate care is being provided.

Even the entrepreneurship that the Tories claim so much to favour is far easier to encourage when there is a strong social safety net. Anyone who gives up his or her job to start a business, or who decides not to seek new employment but to set out independently after losing a job, is inevitably taking a gamble that the venture might fail. But it is a gamble that's in society's best interests to encourage, since start-ups of new businesses have been by far the biggest source of employment growth in Canada over the past decade.

That gamble is far more feasible for an individual to take if he or she knows that in the worst-case scenario — if the business fails and there is temporarily no private source of income — at least the most basic personal and family needs will still be met. Unemployment insurance or welfare will ensure enough money for subsistence, their children will still be able to get a good education without cost, and any family member who falls sick won't be denied the best medical care because of lack of funds. Far from discouraging self-reliance, as right-wingers like to argue, the social safety net helps in this way to create an environment where it can more readily be pursued.

Supportive social policies also help the economy in a broader sense by providing a chance to break the cycle of poverty that otherwise wastes so much human potential and creates social problems of its own. As the experience of the United States has clearly shown, when the disadvantaged are left to feel abandoned by society, they fall ever deeper into poverty and hopelessness. A culture of poverty gets passed on from generation to generation. Young people who might otherwise be productive contributors to the economy and society are left idle and isolated at best, or they turn to crime with its resulting social and economic costs. In the long run, there is no benefit to business — let alone to society at large — from such an outcome. There is only waste, and loss.

Only the most short-sighted or ideologically blink-ered could see some threat to economic efficiency from measures that facilitate labour force flexibility and industrial adjustment, that nurture human resources and leave workers freer to concentrate on their work, that encourage entrepreneurial risk-taking, that help to break the cycle of poverty and unproductiveness, and that spare our cities from becoming crime-ridden battle-grounds. Yet that has been the position of Mulroney and his ministers ever since they came to power. In the name of fighting the deficit, they have consistently argued that our social spending has gotten out of line, and they have eroded one social program after another.

The reality, however, is that of the 24 nations in the Organization for Economic Co-operation and Develop-ment, Canada ranks no higher than 13th in total social spending by all levels of government as a percentage of gross domestic product. Countries that regularly outspend us include France, Germany, the Netherlands, Belgium and Austria.

To the Mulroney government and to the business com-munity, that's irrelevant. The only comparison they care about is to the United States, which does indeed have less social spending — and which pays the consequences, in terms of general quality of life. But no one has yet coherently explained why our level of social spending somehow makes us less competitive, even against the United States. The very idea seems all the more paradox-ical when we consider that the Americans themselves regard some of our key social programs — unemploy-ment insurance and medicare, for instance — as indirect subsidies that give us an unfair competitive *advantage* by reducing the costs that Canadian business must bear.

In any event, it is not at all irrelevant that our social spending is lower than that of nearly every major industrialized country other than the United States. It throws into serious doubt the suggestion that our business community somehow cannot cope with the tax "burden" arising from our traditional levels of social spending. Countries such as Germany, Belgium, France and the Netherlands have had successful, solid economies while devoting a larger proportion of their gross domestic product to social expenditures by government. If their business communities can cope, why can't ours?

The United States has been economically successful while acting in accordance with American values that stress individualism above all else. Other industrialized countries have achieved economic success and a good standard of living while pursuing their own, different mixes of values. So what empowers the Mulroney government and some business leaders to insist that the United States, which may yet pay a steadily heavier economic and social price for its short-sightedness, is the one model we must pattern ourselves after?

If the issue is overdependence on the United States as a trading partner, why haven't the Tories and the corporations pushed for diversifying our trade links instead of enmeshing ourselves ever more tightly through free trade? There are enormous opportunities in the Pacific Rim, in the New Europe and in the developing countries. And if the issue is the deficit itself, why is it social programs — and not, say, tax breaks to big business and the most wealthy — that are being singled out as what we particularly cannot afford, despite their importance not only to fairness but also to long-term economic development and competitiveness?

The Mulroney government has not even attempted to answer such questions. It has simply embarked, in every available way, on a step-by-step dismantling of our social support network, without even providing a coherent rationale for its actions. At a time of soaring unemployment caused largely by their own free trade deal and their own high-interest-rate, high-dollar policies, Mulroney and his team have "reformed" unemployment insurance. They have made it more difficult to be eligible for UI payments, and they have cut back the benefit entitlements of those who do still qualify. In the process, they have hit hardest at the most vulnerable. An estimated 80 per cent of those losing benefits are low-income workers earning less than $25,000 a year.

For Canadians who cannot either support themselves through employment or be sustained by unemployment insurance, the safety net of very last resort is welfare, more formally known as the Canada Assistance Plan (CAP). Having pursued policies that lead inevitably to high unemployment, having implemented changes that throw more of the jobless off unemployment insurance and onto welfare, Mulroney has attacked welfare as well.

The Canada Assistance Plan, established in 1966, was designed as a partnership between the federal government and the provinces to help the poorest of the poor. Under the terms of federal-provincial CAP agreements, all provinces and territories are required to provide financial aid to all residents who are "in need." Need is determined in each individual case by a "needs test" — a detailed assessment of whether an individual's or a family's costs for the bare necessities of life are higher than income from all available sources. In addition to financial help, the Canada Assistance Plan also provides community support services for people on welfare and for those deemed likely to fall onto the welfare rolls were it not for such services.

From the very start in 1966, the agreed role of the national government was to pay half the cost of all expenditures that qualified under the plan. The federal legislation establishing the plan quite deliberately put no dollar limit on the amount of the federal contribution. It was agreed that since welfare is the absolute last resort for people who are financially desperate, the program had to be flexible and open-ended enough to help everyone in that situation at any given time.

But in its February 1990 budget, the Mulroney government suddenly and unilaterally broke that agreement. It announced that for the next two fiscal years, increases in federal payments under the plan to Ontario, Alberta and British Columbia would be arbitrarily limited to 5 per cent a year — no matter how much welfare costs actually increased, amid soaring unemployment and Mulroney's unemployment insurance cutbacks. Any increases above 5 per cent would have to be absorbed by the provincial governments.

The Tories' reasoning was that these three provinces, being Canada's wealthiest, could afford to absorb the shortfall in payments. But they are also provinces that together have nearly half of all Canada's welfare recipients. And all three, but especially Ontario, have economies that are particularly vulnerable to the effects of prolonged recession.

The three provincial governments calculated that Mulroney's two-year ceiling would cost them a total of at least $865 million. But Mulroney wasn't content even with that. His next budget, in February 1991, extended the 5 per cent ceiling for another three years, to the end of 1995. Far from being merely a transfer of costs from one level of government to another, Mulroney's breach of faith is an attack on welfare itself.

Provincial governments do not have limitless funds. They can cope with the financial shortfall by increasing taxes, by increasing their deficits or by restraining welfare payments and services. Taking more money out of the economy during a recession by significantly raising taxes can risk making the recession worse — and throwing still more people onto welfare. When the Ontario government opted instead to increase its deficit somewhat, Mulroney was among the first to attack it for this decision. What his government wants to force, quite evidently, is a curbing of the welfare programs themselves. The long-term impact is unlikely to be limited only to the three provinces directly affected. Although payments to welfare recipients across Canada still leave them far below the poverty line, no provincial government is likely even to contemplate improving benefits or services when it faces the prospect of the federal government reneging on paying its share.

It is scarcely surprising that the National Council of Welfare — the federal government's own official advisory body — sums up the impact of Mulroney's welfare ceiling this way: "Throughout most of its years in power, the current federal government has insisted that one of its prime goals in social policy was to redirect benefits to people most in need. The Minister of Finance abandoned that approach in his 1990 budget by asking — in effect — that the poorest of the poor share the burden of his campaign to cut government spending . . . No previous federal government ever suggested pulling back from its basic commitment to the needs of the poor."

At the same time, Mulroney has also hit hard at the poorest Canadians by eroding the progressiveness of our tax system. Tax changes in successive federal budgets since 1984, combined with corresponding changes in provincial income taxes based on the federal tax, have resulted in the poorest income-earners paying far more than before while the richest are actually paying less. Take the example of a working-poor family with two income earners, two children and total earnings of $20,000. In constant 1989 dollars, that family's total federal and provincial income taxes have soared from $175 in 1984 to $822 in 1991 — an increase of 370 per cent. Over the same period, the total income taxes of a corresponding middle-income family earning $49,000 have increased 17 per cent. And those of an upper-income family earning $123,000 have *dropped* by 6 per cent.

Mulroney has further eroded the progressiveness of our tax system by introducing a major consumption tax, the Goods and Services Tax (GST). By definition, income taxes are progressive, because they are tied to earnings and, hence, ability to pay. Consumption taxes are regressive, because everyone pays the same amount on any given purchase: A parent scraping by on $26,000 a year must pay the same extra $7 in GST on $100 worth of children's clothing as someone earning $100,000.

Along with slashing at unemployment insurance, welfare and the progressiveness of the tax system, the Mulroney government's onslaught against our social support network has also included an assault on the long-established principle of universality in certain key social programs.

Both family allowances and old-age security pensions were designed as universal programs; that is, programs that pay meaningful benefits to every Canadian who meets the basic qualification, without any needs test required. Families with children, and the elderly, automatically qualified for benefits under these programs, regardless of income. The whole point behind universality has been that it provides a way for our society, through the national government, to recognize the contribution that *all* parents make by raising children, and that *all* the elderly have made throughout their lives.

Whenever anyone in the past suggested tampering with universality, there was a great public outcry from Canadians who regard it as a fundamental element of our social policy. Indeed, Mulroney himself vowed in the House of Commons on December 20, 1984: "We are going to protect the integrity of universality in this country. I will guarantee it." That guarantee evaporated in the April 1989 federal budget, when Mulroney's government effectively ended universality with a gimmick known as the "clawback." Everybody would continue to receive family allowance and old-age pensions — but those with incomes above a certain amount wouldn't get to *keep* a penny of it. Then, in the February 1992 Budget, the Tory government ended the universality of family allowances altogether.

The clawback mechanism, a back-door assault on universality, remains in place for old-age pensions. Under the provisions of the 1989 budget, pension recipients must pay back to the government, at tax time, 15 per cent of their benefits for every dollar of income over $50,000. While $50,000 is by no means a modest income, the clawback mechanism is only partially indexed for inflation. This means that in years ahead, when our incomes rise in dollar terms but our buying power remains virtually unchanged — when $50,000 is worth $40,000 — more and more relatively modest income earners will be "clawed." Increasing numbers of middle-income Canadians will no longer be able to count on meaningful old-age security payments for their retirement years.

Then there's the broader issue of the merits of universality itself. The argument against giving social benefits to the comparatively well-off, rather than just to the needy, is certainly superficially persuasive. But a distinctive feature of the Canadian social support system has been precisely that social programs are not solely "for the poor." Because everyone has been touched by at least one universal program — family allowance, old-age pension, medicare — there has been less of an us-versus-them feeling about social programs generally than in many other countries. We Canadians have seen social policy as something our entire community does for itself in our own self-interest, rather than as just something the rich do for the poor.

Because everyone has some exposure to social programs, we have an early warning system to alert us to governments that seek to erode our most basic and fundamental Canadian values. The Canada Assistance Plan is so far removed from the experience of the majority of people that any tampering a government might do with welfare could go unfelt. It would seem abstract and remote to them. But because most people have at least some personal stake in family allowances, old-age pensions or unemployment insurance, negative changes in these programs serve to alert us that the government is insensitive toward social policy.

In a way, universality serves the same function in protecting social programs as a canary served in protecting coal miners. If the canary keeled over dead, the miners knew that poisonous gas was seeping toward them. If the programs that touch the great majority of Canadians start being eroded, we know that the most vulnerable are probably being shafted as well. And retaining the capacity to arouse the middle class — whether out of self-interest or out of caring for others, in any given instance — is crucial to safeguarding our social safety net.

The poor themselves are relatively powerless in political terms. They don't have the numbers, or the voice, to bring down a government. It is only by ensuring that the great majority of Canadians — the middle class — will have the awareness and the motivation to make common cause with them, that we can ensure we remain the kind of society most Canadians want us to be.

Nowhere is the Mulroney government's attack on universal social programs more acute, or more socially dangerous, than in the case of medicare. The whole point of medicare, since its inception, has been to ensure that every Canadian without exception can have full access to the same quality of medical care, without any regard to income. It was correctly determined that the only way to actually accomplish this objective is to eliminate all direct financial transactions between patient and physician.

That's because even seemingly small direct payments for medical care — whether in the form of user fees, deterrent fees to discourage unnecessary visits, or extra-billing by specialists — have an effect on people of modest income that they do not have on the more affluent. The reality is that deterrent fees will deter only those who can ill afford them, and user fees will restrict use only by those for whom money is tight.

A parent earning $60,000 isn't likely to think twice about paying $5 or $10 to take a child with a sore throat or an earache to the doctor, just to be on the safe side. But someone with three children and an income of only $30,000 might well feel cause to wait longer under the same circumstances, because $5 or $10 every time can quickly add up. And if the sore throat turned out to be strep, or the earache was a serious infection, the delay in getting medical care might lead to the child being sicker than necessary, or even lastingly affected. Similarly, the prospect of ending up paying several hundred dollars for a hospital stay might cause some people to delay or avoid having necessary surgery, while the more affluent would go ahead and be the healthier for it.

If we allow that to happen, we will be sacrificing not only fairness but also good sense. Much is known these days about the importance of preventive medicine, about how much easier — and hence more cost-effective — it is to treat medical problems when they are discovered early than when they have already become acute. In the long run, we are likely to have not only a healthier population, but lower health-care costs, if we do not discourage people from seeking medical attention when they have a concern. Even if some of the visits turn out to have been unnecessary, the cost is likely to be outweighed by the savings from those others that catch a problem before it requires more extensive and expensive treatment.

In any event, the issue isn't whether any given medical consultation actually turns out to be necessary or not, or whether a hospital stay is truly urgent. It is, rather, that once money considerations make some people hesitate while the richer needn't think twice, the most fun-

damental — and most attractive — principle of medicare will have been destroyed.

That is precisely what the Mulroney government has
begun to do. Through a succession of unilateral cutbacks since 1986, the Mulroney government has steadily reduced the contribution to health-care and post-secondary education costs it was committed to making
under the Established Programs Financing Act of 1977.
That legislation provided that federal financial support
would grow at the same rate as the growth rate of the
Canadian economy as a whole. But in 1986 the Tories
declared that the federal contribution would increase by
two percentage points *less* than the rate of growth of the
economy. In the 1989 budget, they cut back further, to
three percentage points less than the economic growth
rate. In the 1990 budget, they announced a total two-
year freeze in the level of the contribution. And in 1991,
they extended the total freeze for another two years, to
be followed by a return to the formula of three percentage points less than economic growth.

According to calculations by the National Council of
Welfare, these changes reduced the federal contribution
for the 1991–92 fiscal year alone by $4 billion — or near-
ly 17 per cent — from what it would otherwise have
been. Over the period from the start of the cutbacks in
1986 until 1999, the total reduction will amount to $97.6
billion — or roughly 22 per cent.

Such huge shortfalls put enormous financial pressure
on provincial governments, particularly on those of the
least affluent provinces. That pressure will push the
provinces in the direction of cutting back on health services or finding alternative ways to help fund the system — ways such as user fees and extra-billing. The

most likely outcome is some combination of both cut-backs and imposition of costs directly on patients.

At the same time, Mulroney's Tories are also deliberately dismantling the only instrument possessed by the federal government to maintain national standards or prevent direct charges to patients within medicare. The delivery of health care is exclusively within provincial jurisdiction. But the federal government has the explicit power, under the Canada Health Act of 1984, to enforce the principles of medicare by withholding its cash payments for health care if a province imposes out-of-pocket costs on patients or otherwise erodes the program. That, of course, can work only if there are cash payments to withhold in the first place. And so the Mulroney government is phasing out cash payments. Under the Established Programs Financing Act, the federal contribution is made up partly of cash payments and partly of tax transfers to the provinces. That is, the federal government lowered its tax rate by a certain number of percentage points, and each provincial government raised its rate by a corresponding percentage. The federal cash payments each year are only for the shortfall between the amount provinces raise through the tax transfer and the total federal contribution owing.

The result of systematically cutting back the federal contribution is that an ever smaller share of the total is in the form of cash payments. The National Council of Welfare estimates that under present trends, the cash payments will have disappeared altogether by 2008. As those payments dwindle and then disappear, of course, the federal government will have nothing to withhold and hence no way of maintaining a cohesive national health-care system. There is, however, no evidence that the Tories would want to do so anyway. At a federal Progressive Conservative policy convention in the summer of 1991, a majority of the party voted in favour of seeing the introduction of user fees under medicare.

The prospect, if what Mulroney and his Tories have set in motion is allowed to continue, is the gradual collapse of medicare as we know it. Without the carrot and stick of direct federal funding, each province will increasingly go its own way in deciding what medical services will be covered and what costs patients must bear. Instead of a national system in which medical care with no out-of-pocket charges is the birthright of every Canadian, everywhere from coast to coast, we will revert to a patchwork of vastly different systems. And if user fees and extra-billing are allowed to take hold, we are likely to revert as well to a situation where the kind of health care we receive depends on the size of our bank account. At one end of the income spectrum, the affluent will be able to get extra attention, faster care or much readier access to top-notch specialists by paying substantial additional fees. At the other end, as user fees and extra-billing become more widespread and costlier, either the poorest of the poor will be exempted — and thus identified as poor every time they seek medical care — or separate clinics and hospitals will be developed to meet their needs. Either way, we are likely to end up with an income-segmented health-care system as in the United States or in Britain.

There is no reason, other than ideology, for the Mulroney government to be setting us on this course. It is simply not true that the federal government's health-care costs had been soaring out of control. In 1985, just before Mulroney started his cutbacks, the federal government's

health-care costs actually accounted for a lower proportion of total government spending than they had five
years earlier: 6 per cent in 1985 compared to 7.1 per cent
in 1980. In fact, health-care spending by *all* levels of
government — federal, provincial and municipal — as a
proportion of total government spending was virtually
unchanged over the entire decade between 1975 and
1985. It accounted for 12.4 per cent in 1975 and 12.2 per
cent in 1985. Since then, health care's share of total
spending has increased by less than a percentage point.

Even comparisons to the United States — the favourite
basis for Tory and business community claims that we
cannot afford our social support network — show not the
slightest foundation for arguing that we overspend on
health care. We spend less than 9 percent of Canada's total
gross domestic product on health-care. The Americans
spend more than 12 per cent. There is growing pressure
in the United States, indeed, to adopt a health-care system patterned on our medicare.

If provincial governments have been complaining
lately about soaring health-care costs, the main reason is
not that something has suddenly gone wrong with the
health-care system itself. The annual per capita increase
in the cost of medicare, adjusted for inflation, has been
slightly less than the 4 per cent projected by the Hall
Royal Commission, which recommended the system in
1965. The main problem, rather, is that the Mulroney
government's failure to pay its share has put enormous
pressure on provincial treasuries.

This does not mean that there is no room for improvements in the cost-efficiency of delivering health care.
Such improvements can and should be pursued. But
there is no need, and no justification, for eroding either

the principles or the cohesiveness of a medicare system that has been the envy of much of the world and the pride of Canadians.

The same is true of our social safety net as a whole. In working to dismantle the social support structure and the sense of community that underlies it, Mulroney has been striking not only at programs, not only at fairness, not only at the well-being of individual citizens. The ultimate victim of his policies has been something even more fundamental. He has been assailing, and deeply wounding, our understanding of who we are as Canadians and what makes our country special and profoundly worth preserving.

Not-So-Free Trade

THROUGHOUT OUR HISTORY, Canadians have made a deliberate act of the will to keep our nation independent and distinctive in the shadow of a neighbour ten times our size. Brian Mulroney's Canada–U.S. free trade deal is a deliberate act of the will, by our own government, to do the opposite by signing away the sovereignty that should be the birthright of our children.

Far from being merely a bad trade deal that is already devastating our economy, the 1988 agreement strikes directly at our long-term ability to control our own destiny as Canadians. It effectively signs away our right to make our own autonomous decisions in nearly every important field, including energy and natural resources, economic development, social policy, environmental protection, safety and consumer protection standards and culture.

And those are only the direct, contractual effects of the deal. The indirect effect, which we already see happening, is to give rise to a constant, unyielding pressure to become more like the United States in every way.

The consequences of all this are already having an impact on our national psyche. Even Canadians who are not familiar with the details of free trade have a growing sense that the country has been profoundly altered, that the Canada they know is being swallowed up by American control and American values, and that they are helpless to do anything about it.

None of this is any accident. It is a direction knowingly imposed on Canada by Mulroney, who himself had said of free trade during the 1983 Tory leadership campaign: "It affects Canadian sovereignty and we will have none of it, not during leadership campaigns or any other time . . . This country could not survive with a policy of unfettered free trade. We'd be swamped. All that would happen with that kind of concept would be the boys cranking up their plants throughout the United States in bad times and shutting their entire branch plants in Canada. It's bad enough as it is."

And Quebec Premier Robert Bourassa, who later became Mulroney's key ally in defending free trade in the 1988 federal election, had also been saying as recently as February 1986: "Free trade with the United States will inevitably threaten Canada's political sovereignty. Canadians must be made aware of the dangers that lie ahead if Prime Minister Brian Mulroney leads us into an all-out free trade agreement with the Americans . . . We can't separate economic integration from political integration."

The immediate economic effects of the deal have been as predictable as they have been ruinous. As our border is flung unrestrictedly open to imports from the United States, many U.S.–owned industries no longer perceive any reason to serve the Canadian market from within Canada. The deal invites them to decide it would be far more cost-efficient to shut down their Canadian plants, increase their production runs in the United States by 10 per cent and ship their goods into Canada. By the same token, even Canadian-owned companies have an incentive to move their plants to parts of the United States that have cheaper labour and are closer to the geographic centre of the North American market.

As if this were not already a sufficient blueprint for ravaging the Canadian economy, Mulroney and his Tories have since 1988 been making the situation infinitely worse by cranking up interest rates and the value of the Canadian dollar. They have simultaneously flung us into an unprotected competitive duel against American businesses, and ensured we would be incapable of winning that duel. The excessively high value of our dollar automatically prices many of our exports out of the market in the United States, while making U.S. exports into Canada a much more competitive purchase.

While the combination of free trade and a high Canadian dollar is nothing short of lethal for our economy, it is difficult to believe the United States would have been willing to sign the deal without some sort of commitment from the Mulroney government to keep our dollar high. Mulroney's ministers have always denied there was any such under-the-table agreement, but logic suggests otherwise. At the dollar's previous value in the 70- to 75-cent range, our goods had a competitive advantage in the U.S. market. It would have been entirely contrary to the negotiating style of the American side to agree to a deal that would have allowed us to maintain that advantage, or even increase it by dropping the dollar further still.

In one sense, whether there was such an agreement about the dollar scarcely matters: Either Mulroney promised the Americans, as a secret part of the free trade deal, to cripple our economy by committing us to a dollar level that would render us uncompetitive. Or his government spontaneously surrendered Canadian businesses to their American competitors through a high-dollar policy after the fact, without even having had any negotiating reason to do so. Either way, the consequences are the same.

In the 21 months between June 1989 and March 1991 alone, Canada lost as many as 435,000 manufacturing jobs — a loss of more than 20 per cent of total manufacturing employment. Canadians can readily see that we are in the throes of something far more fundamental and lasting than just another cyclical recession. These are jobs that for the most part are gone forever as factories are bankrupted or relocate.

Canadians are left with a sense that our economy is beginning to crumble and that we are being abandoned to fend for ourselves as best we can amid the economic rubble. Those who have lost their jobs have not been given the retraining or adjustment assistance that Mulroney had so solemnly promised when he announced the trade deal. And while this undermining of our industrial base is destructive enough in itself, what is even worse is the way Mulroney's trade deal has signed away our right as Canadians to manage our own affairs in our own best interest.

Our vital resources — including oil, gas, electricity, lumber and minerals — are no longer ours to do with as we please. One of Canada's greatest competitive advantages has been our riches in natural resources, and hence our freedom to give Canadian industries preferential access to those resources at lower than world prices. Secure and comparatively cheap resource supplies, even at times of global scarcity, can make it possible for our manufactured exports to be cheaper than those of other countries. But the Mulroney trade deal wipes out those benefits in our dealings with our biggest competitor. Even though they are *our* resources, developed with our tax dollars, we are forbidden under the deal to benefit from our ownership and investment by choosing to sell energy or other resources cheaper to Canadians than to the United States.

Mulroney has even given away our right to ensure that we have enough of an energy resource to meet our own needs before we export any of it. In times of shortage such as the oil supply crisis of the 1970s, we are no longer free to use Canadian resources to meet Canadian needs first and then export whatever is left over. Under Mulroney's deal, we are committed to guaranteeing the United States the same share of the total supply as before there was a shortage. Canadian oil would have to flow to help keep the United States supplied, even if that ultimately meant some Canadian homes would have to go unheated or some industries that employ Canadians would have to shut down.

Even our water is covered under this provision. If Canada ever yields to ongoing U.S. pressure to begin large-scale water exports — as some are already advocating — the proportional-sharing provision means we will never again be able to turn off the tap afterward, even if we become concerned about adequacy of supply for our own needs or about environmental impact. Our children, or our children's children, could conceivably run short of fresh water some day because Brian Mulroney concocted a trade deal that tells the Americans that what's theirs is theirs, and what's ours is theirs too.

Mulroney has likewise signed away our freedom to shape Canada's economic development or even to ensure that businesses in Canada operate for the benefit of Canadians. Various provisions of the deal will make it virtually impossible for future Canadian governments to develop an effective national industrial strategy. In fact, our hands are tied in terms of even protecting what already exists.

When American corporations want to buy up Canadian companies, in most instances we no longer have the right to make sure it's a good deal for Canada. The free trade pact raises the company value at which foreign takeovers become subject to review by Investment Canada from $5 million to $150 million. This means that only takeovers of a few hundred of the largest companies, instead of the thousands previously covered, can even be examined by an investment review body.

Even then, we no longer have the right to impose performance requirements on investors. We can no longer say that you cannot buy an important Canadian company unless you are going to create more jobs for Canadians, rather than lay off Canadian workers and transfer their jobs to the United States. We can no longer say that you cannot buy a Canadian company unless you are going to have it do research and development work in Canada with Canadian talent, not just at head office south of the border. And we can no longer say that some parts of the Canadian economy that are the key to our future — like our major financial institutions or our leading high-tech companies, for instance — are just plain off limits to foreign buyers.

Mulroney's trade deal has also failed to protect our right to continue our regional development policies. These policies reflect fundamental Canadian values by helping the less advantaged parts of Canada, such as the Atlantic provinces, to share in our prosperity by developing new business activities. But the Americans have long seen the whole range of regional development programs as unfair trade subsidies. And now we are committed under the agreement to a negotiated "harmonization" of our approach to subsidies with that of the United States.

Similarly, Mulroney has surrendered our ability to use government procurement as an instrument of economic development. Under the deal the federal government, and probably eventually provincial governments, no longer have the right to give small Canadian firms a break and a chance to grow by buying goods and "goods-related services" from them rather than from big American corporations. The deal provides that a corporation headquartered in Atlanta or Dallas or New York has to be given exactly the same chance to get most government business as a company owned by Canadians for Canadians — no more local preferences. In a country where all levels of government spend a total of more than $70 billion a year on buying goods and services, Mulroney has given up our right to spend Canadian tax money in ways that create business opportunities and jobs for Canadians rather than for others.

But while stripping Canada of virtually all its economic development instruments, Mulroney has agreed to let the Americans keep their most powerful one entirely intact and, indeed, undiscussed. The United States hides its main industrial subsidy system under the cloak of national security. It uses its massive national defence spending as an extremely potent system of industrial subsidy and regional development. Government con-

tracts to companies that produce goods whose application is far from exclusively military — everything from
machinery to toilet seats — give these firms a financial
boost that lets them undercut foreign competitors. Yet
Mulroney has agreed, absurdly, that national defence
spending — which plays a much less important role in
Canada — be exempted from the deal.

It isn't just the interests of Canadian companies and
workers that Mulroney has surrendered. It's our whole
distinctive Canadian way of doing things, our commitment to using direct government involvement to accomplish for the public benefit what the private sector will
not or cannot do. The Americans don't understand this
approach. To them, it is nothing more than interference
with free market forces. It is inconceivable, for instance,
to imagine in the United States a publicly owned, government-owned broadcasting network like the CBC or a
government-owned airline like Air Canada was before
Mulroney privatized it.

Under the trade deal, we are no longer free to meet
new national needs with new Crown corporations or comprehensive public-sector programs. The deal describes
such initiatives solely from the American point of view, as
"designating a monopoly." And it says we can't ever do it
again without first getting permission from Washington,
to make sure we're not hurting the interests of any
American businesses. If American firms do object, we
will either be prohibited from going ahead or have to pay
them "prompt, adequate and effective compensation" for
any future profits they would be losing.

That would make it virtually impossible, for example,
to ever set up a comprehensive non-profit national day-
care program if Canadians decided that was the best

way to proceed. The deal gives big American child-care companies — like all U.S. service industry firms — an unrestricted right to set up business anywhere in Canada on exactly the same basis as Canadians. If the federal government or a provincial government wanted to set up an exclusively publicly funded, non-profit child-care program, interfering with the right of the American companies to come in and make a buck, this would be considered a "monopoly" under the deal. We would have to go hat in hand to Washington for permission to do what we would normally perceive as a Canadian right. If we were allowed to proceed at all, it would be on condition of "compensating" U.S. companies for the potential future profits they'd be losing. That could run into billions of dollars. We would, in effect, have to pay for day care twice: once for the actual cost of providing the care, and again to American companies for *not* providing it. The costs would obviously be unaffordable, thwarting the whole idea. The same holds true for any other future public sector programs we might contemplate, from dental care to auto insurance.

Our existing social programs — or what's left of them after Mulroney's cutbacks and clawbacks — are also at risk. The Americans have long insisted that many of these programs, including unemployment insurance and medicare, are unacceptable subsidies. Under the deal, Mulroney has agreed that Canada and the United States will negotiate over the next few years which of our programs and policies constitute unfair subsidies that justify American retaliation unless we abandon them. What kind of negotiation will that be? We already know what the Americans think, and Mulroney has already demonstrated his bargaining prowess by giving away virtually everything else they wanted while gaining nothing in return. The prospect is that, yet again, they will call the tune and we will "harmonize."

The deal also binds Canada to "harmonize" our policies in a range of other fields, including the environment and safety and consumer protection standards, with those of the United States. "Harmonize" is defined in the agreement as to make the same or make identical. It doesn't take much imagination to deduce what will happen if we harmonize our environmental policies with those of a country that took years to admit that there even exists such a thing as acid rain. Nor is the outcome for Canadians in doubt if we set out to make our safety or consumer protection standards the same as those of a country that has generally less rigorous standards and enforces them to a lesser degree.

Our freedom in the cultural field, although supposedly exempt from the free trade agreement, is also effectively curtailed. For Canadians, our books, magazines, music, movies, plays and art are a crucial means of expressing our distinctive identity, communicating with one another, and fostering national pride. To U.S. trade officials, on the other hand, culture is just another commodity. American cultural industries are a major component of their national economy, and selling American culture to the world is an enormous source of export revenues.

In the trade deal, Mulroney accepts the U.S. view of culture as primarily an object of trade, and he thereby puts our cultural sovereignty gravely at risk. The same article of the deal that exempts cultural industries also goes on to specify: "Notwithstanding any other provision of the Agreement, a Party may take measures of equivalent commercial effect in response to action that would have been inconsistent with the agreement but for [the exemption]." In other words, we're free to do what we want in the cultural field — but the deal gives the Americans permission to punish us with economic retaliation if they don't like what we do. And what the United States has historically disliked is any measure — such as Canadian content requirements or preferential tax breaks to Canadian publishers or film-makers — designed to help our comparatively fragile cultural industries from being swamped by the sheer volume and power of U.S. exports. That means the agreement effectively curtails our ability to contemplate any such new initiatives in the future, because retaliation would be inevitable and virtually impossible to appeal.

Beyond its curtailment of our sovereignty in nearly every domain, the deal is already inflicting a terrible toll on our national psyche. Our sense of identity was based in large measure on being different and independent from the United States. The shared will to resist the magnetic pull on our southern border was a powerful unifying force. Now we are told, by the deal and by its proponents, that we must give up our distinctly Canadian approach to governing ourselves and adopt instead the American way. We are contractually bound to harmonize and homogenize ourselves. And thus we are stripped of much of our grasp on who and what we are.

For all the evisceration Mulroney's trade deal has inflicted on our economy, our historic approach to the role of government, our sovereignty and our national identity, we have obtained remarkably little in return. Certainly, Mulroney's stated main objective in pursuing free trade in the first place — guaranteed access to the United States market for our exports — has not been attained. He himself had stated that objective, at the outset, in no uncertain terms: "U.S. trade laws can't apply to Canada, period."

Yet U.S. trade laws do still apply, under the deal Mulroney nevertheless accepted. The Americans retain full rights to impose retaliatory sanctions under those laws, in the form of import duties that tax our products out of competitiveness, whenever they deem that we are competing unfairly. All we have obtained is a Canada–U.S. dispute-settling mechanism to establish whether the United States is acting according to its *own* laws in any given instance. If so, they are free to punish us. Since the problem remains that the U.S. trade laws can define subsidies or other unfair trade practices any way the Americans choose, we have really gained nothing at all.

Instead, our own government has made us the only country in modern history that, without having been conquered in war or otherwise compelled to do so, has willingly signed away to a foreign nation effective control over its internal decision-making powers and indeed its whole future.

Fathers of Deconfederation

WHEN THE MULRONEY GOVERNMENT came to power, the national unity debate was dormant in Quebec for the first time in years. Brian Mulroney's singular contribution was to come into a calm situation, stir up a sense of resentment where none had vividly existed, fan it into a full-blown crisis and then prove utterly incapable of resolving the explosive mess he himself had created.

While Quebec's nationalistic political elites had been predictably irate, the 1982 Constitution had won a remarkable degree of acceptance from the province's general population. A Gallup Poll taken on December 10, 1981, at the time the Trudeau government's constitutional initiative was completed, found that only 34 per cent of Quebecers agreed with separatist premier René Lévesque's refusal to sign the new constitutional deal, 46 per cent disagreed and 20 per cent had no opinion.

By the time of the 1984 federal election, with the Lévesque government already on its last legs, the Constitution was the last thing on the minds of most Quebecers. They were ready, for the first time in decades, to turn their attention fully to other concerns, at least for a while.

It was Mulroney who quite deliberately set out to stir up trouble, working systematically to instil in the minds of Quebecers that they had been humiliated by the 1982 Constitution. He launched a campaign to spread this message as early as his speech to his nomination meeting in Sept-Îles in August 1984, when he said: "Not one Quebecer authorized the federal Liberals to take advantage of the confusion that prevailed in Quebec following the referendum to ostracize the province constitutionally. My party takes no pleasure in the politically weak position in which these events have placed Quebec . . . The men and women of this province have undergone a collective trauma."

It was a remarkable statement for someone who had himself supported the Trudeau government's actions on the Constitution. But in 1984 Mulroney was determined to break the Liberal party's long-standing hold on Quebec in federal politics. And to do this, he was prepared to persuade Quebecers that they had been betrayed and isolated by the Liberals, even if that meant also telling them in effect that they had been betrayed and isolated by the rest of Canada itself. To revive a Toryparty that had been virtually non-existent in the province, he was also willing to form an unholy alliance with Quebec's separatist and ultranationalist elements in search of strong candidates and organizational support.

Mulroney was undeterred by the grave threat such a strategy was sure to pose to national unity. He was well aware of that threat, having himself criticized Joe Clark during the leadership campaign: "To try to curry the favour of the Parti Québécois organization during a leadership campaign is dangerous to the candidate who does it, it's dangerous for the future of the party he seeks to lead, and it's dangerous to the future of the united country he seeks to govern."

The most immediate result of Mulroney's political alliance with separatists — even more dangerous, evidently, in a national election than in a leadership campaign — was to muzzle his government in its ability to speak for Canada within Quebec. There were separatists and ultranationalists in his cabinet, in his caucus and throughout the party organization in the province. Saying or doing anything that displeased them would have risked splitting the government wide open.

And so for the first time in history, Canada had a prime minister and a national government unwilling to speak out forcefully against separatism within Quebec, to vigorously argue the case for federalism or even to defend Canada against its critics. Advocates of the break-up of Canada were left with a clear track to shape public opinion in Quebec, leaving ordinary Quebecers to think that their claims must be true if even the federal government couldn't dispute them. Indeed, Mulroney was actively *helping* the fading separatist movement, giving it a new lease on life by telling Quebecers they had been badly treated by the rest of Canada.

Mulroney's Quebec strategy led him not only to reopen old wounds and stir up new resentments, but to prematurely and recklessly reopen the Pandora's box of constitutional amendment. A Conservative government under his leadership, he pledged, would urgently relaunch constitutional negotiations and come up with a deal that Quebec's national assembly would be proud to sign.

That would have enabled him to claim "success" where Trudeau had "failed," while cementing Tory support in Quebec for years to come.

In pursuit of this strategy, in 1987 Mulroney negotiated with the premiers the Meech Lake Accord — an improvised package of constitutional changes that would have radically altered the very nature of Canada, without even the most rudimentary analysis of the likely impacts and without justification of each change on its own merits.

Under the accord's provisions, the entire Constitution was to be interpreted "in a manner consistent with the recognition that Quebec constitutes, within Canada, a distinct society." And the legislature and government of Quebec were to be constitutionally mandated "to preserve and promote this distinct identity."

As Quebec premier Robert Bourassa was quick to triumphantly point out, these provisions added up to an open-ended transfer of powers from the federal government to that of Quebec: "The exercise of legislative authority is included, and we will thus be able to consolidate existing positions and make new gains." Whenever the Quebec government wanted to step into some previously federal area of jurisdiction, it would have been able to claim that the new powers were necessary and justified under the "distinct society" provisions. If the Supreme Court agreed, the federal government would have been weakened that much more each time, and Quebec would have turned that much further inward. If the Supreme Court rejected a given demand, the Quebec government would have claimed to have been thwarted on a crucial matter — and we would have been plunged into new confrontation. The whole provision was, in short, a recipe for separation by degrees.

Every other provision of the accord was designed, as well, to transfer power from the national government to the provinces. The judges of the Supreme Court, which is the ultimate arbiter of all constitutional questions, were henceforth to be selected by provincial governments rather than by the prime minister. Particularly with a set of constitutional provisions as unclear in meaning as those in the accord, such an arrangement was a virtually certain way of guaranteeing that all ambiguities about the division of powers would in future be resolved in favour of the provinces, not in favour of the federal government. The Senate, too, was henceforth to be provincially selected, while retaining its absolute power to veto all legislation passed by the House of Commons — a provision tantamount, in effect, to putting the national government under provincial trusteeship. The federal spending power, under which the national government had been able to initiate great national programs such as medicare in areas of provincial jurisdiction, was to be drastically curtailed. And all future constitutional amendments were to require unanimous agreement by all the provinces, ensuring that only amendments further weakening the central government would realistically have a chance of passing.

The combined effect of all these changes would have been to transform Canada from a country that was already highly decentralized but still had a national government strong enough to be effective, into one where the federal government increasingly became little more than a secretariat to carry out the wishes of the provinces.

Canadians were never asked whether they wanted their country reshaped in this way. They were never told how any of the proposed changes were supposed to make

Canada better, fairer or easier to govern in the best interests of ordinary people. They were simply told that was how it had to be, whether they liked it or not. Incredibly, the premiers and the prime minister even formally bound themselves in the agreement not to change a word or a comma of the constitutional package, no matter what flaws might be found on closer examination or what public opinion might say. The nation's Constitution, the fundamental law that belongs to all the people and is meant to express our common will, was literally being hijacked at the instigation of our own prime minister.

By Quebec premier Robert Bourassa's own admission, none of this was necessary. There had been no crisis, no emergency, no burning sense of urgency on the part of Quebec's people or government. "We could have waited until next year," he said in May 1987. "We could have waited until after the next federal election. We were under no pressure. I was serene. But when I saw that it was falling to us, piece by piece, I said to myself, 'Voilà, there it is.'"

Yet when Canadians began to understand the implications of the constitutional package and to speak out against it, Mulroney deliberately raised the stakes. In an attempt to bully the public into accepting the accord and the premiers into ratifying it amid mounting opposition, the prime minister set about creating a crisis atmosphere. The polls at this point showed that most Quebecers were unaware of the content of the Meech Lake Accord and scarcely in a frenzy of excitement as to its fate. But Mulroney repeated over and over that any rejection of Meech Lake — for any reason whatever — would be the ultimate slap in the face to a Quebec already brutalized by the 1982 Constitution.

"We must never forget that, in 1982, Quebec was left alone, isolated and humiliated," he said in one of his typical sorties. "How could we, for a single moment, accept Quebec being excluded from national life? It was the worst injustice ever inflicted on Quebecers." On another occasion, Mulroney said: "If Queen's Park and the people of Ontario had said, 'We don't want this Constitution,' do you think the Queen would have come over here and there would have been a party in front of Parliament Hill with everybody in striped pants celebrating a Constitution without the industrial heartland of Ontario?"

With the prime minister of Canada telling Quebecers that they were "owed" the Meech Lake Accord and would be suffering the ultimate rejection by Canada if it failed to pass, Premier Bourassa was only too happy to take up the same themes. Soon both men were warning that failure to ratify the accord could lead to the break-up of Canada. And Quebec separatists, having initially rejected the accord as giving Quebec far too little, found it expedient to join the chorus. If Meech Lake had eventually passed, they would have mocked it as mere crumbs. But a rejection of the accord, they were now able to say, would mean by the Canadian prime minister's own admission that the rest of Canada rejected Quebec.

Mulroney's incendiary antics soon had a predictable enough effect. If their own prime minister tells people often enough that they have been "ostracized," "traumatized," "isolated" and "humiliated," they will eventually start to believe it. Before long, what had begun as a manufactured crisis had become a very real one. Quebecers started to feel resentful, nationalist sentiments became widespread and the fate of the Meech

Lake Accord was increasingly seen as a make-or-break test of the rest of Canada's good will.

Having almost single-handedly created this explosive situation in Quebec, Mulroney simultaneously managed through his tactics to stir up a dangerous backlash in other provinces. Canadians had not seen the 1982 Constitution as any kind of anti-Quebec gesture, but merely as a refusal to be stymied by a then-separatist government that could scarcely have been expected to endorse a commitment to Canada. But suddenly the prime minister was telling us we had no choice but to atone for this by transforming our country in ways that seemed both objectionable and unnecessary. Otherwise, Quebec might separate. To many it seemed like black-mail, and feelings began to harden — both against the accord itself and against the threat of Quebec separa-tion. These reactions, in turn, made Quebecers feel all the more alienated and rejected, and the vicious circle continued its downward spiral.

It was a situation aggravated beyond measure by Mulroney's failure even to articulate, let alone uphold, the traditional Canadian determination to resolve con-flicts through compromise. Instead of accepting propos-als to address some of the very legitimate concerns about provisions of the accord, and urging Bourassa to do like-wise, Mulroney sided entirely with the Quebec premier in insisting that absolutely no substantive changes could be made. It had to be all or nothing. Since all-or-nothing has never been the Canadian way, it is scarcely surpris-ing that the whole exercise ultimately collapsed and that nothing is what Mulroney ended up with.

When the accord did fail, Mulroney's previous tactics left him unable to meet his responsibilities, as prime

minister, to try to mitigate the damage to public opinion
in Quebec. Having insisted up to the very last moment,
in increasingly apocalyptic tones, that failure would be a
total disaster, Mulroney had no fall-back position. He
didn't even try to tell Quebecers that the failure of
Meech Lake was not the end of the world after all,
merely one setback like others before it on the long
road of constitutional evolution. He simply lapsed into a
prolonged silence, leaving separatists to do their worst
and others to try to pick up the pieces as best they
could.

Then, in October 1991, Mulroney put forward a new
package of constitutional proposals — a package that
was in many respects even worse than the Meech Lake
Accord. The scope of the "distinct society" provision
had been somewhat narrowed. But the thrust of the new
package was an even more wholesale transfer of federal
powers to the provinces than in the accord, coupled
with an attempt to lock into our Constitution key elements of the right-wing Tory agenda.

In the midst of a deep recession and soaring unemployment caused in large measure by the ruinous Tory
policy of high interest rates and a high Canadian dollar,
Mulroney had the temerity to propose constitutionally
obliging the Bank of Canada to carry out that policy forever. Without explanation or justification — certainly
without any province having asked for it — Mulroney
and his government came out of the blue with their proposal to constitutionally entrench inflation-fighting as
the sole mandate of the Bank of Canada.

That is nothing less than a proposal to constitutionally
guarantee high unemployment. Whenever the central
bank focuses exclusively on inflation, as it has done

throughout the Mulroney years, it does so at the expense
of other fundamentally important objectives of economic
policy. Promoting economic growth and maximizing
employment for Canadians are at least equally important,
yet both fall by the wayside when inflation is the only tar-
get. Inflation-fighters insist a high-valued dollar is necessary to keep down the price of imports, which otherwise
would be inflationary. But the same high dollar raises the
price of Canadian exports to levels where they cannot
compete, killing jobs in Canada. And high interest rates,
defended as necessary to keep the value of the dollar high,
themselves kill economic growth and throw Canadians out
of work. Particularly in the context of the free trade
agreement with the United States, this is a prescription
for economic suicide.

Equally from out of nowhere and unrelated to current
needs and demands came Mulroney's proposal to
entrench "property rights" in the Constitution. This has
long been a big favourite of right-wingers, since the
unrestricted right to own and use property however one
sees fit can be used to defend everything from environmental destructiveness to discrimination to possession
of firearms.

If flinging these new and controversial elements into
the constitutional mix for no apparent reason at such a
sensitive time might seem bizarre, it is nevertheless
entirely consistent with Mulroney's whole approach to
the Quebec issue. First he created a crisis where none
existed, to suit his own partisan ends. Then he told
Canadians that because there was a crisis, we had no
choice but to accept his constitutional proposals without
change. That having failed and having provoked an
even greater crisis, it is scarcely out of character for

Mulroney to try to use that crisis as cover under which to ram through elements of his own ideological agenda.

The inescapable reality, of course, is that Canada cannot be strengthened by weakening it. National unity cannot be enhanced by dismantling the capacity of the central government to lead in the pursuit of common purposes that bind us together. And Quebecers cannot be encouraged to feel more fully a part of Canada by the devising of constitutional ways for Quebec to feel as little a part of Canada as possible. This is where, indeed, the whole thrust of all the Mulroney government's policies since 1984 — all the program-slashing, deregulation and privatization — has added impetus to separatist pressures in Quebec. By weakening the benefits of being Canadian — the social safety net, the dedication to fairness, the pursuit of policies that benefit ordinary people, the shared endeavour to build an ever better country for ourselves and our children — Mulroney and his team have understandably weakened the attraction to Quebecers of remaining part of Canada.

Quebecers, even more than Canadians in other provinces, need to be able to feel strongly that Canada *is* special, or the appeal of a nationalism based on their own language and culture becomes all the more difficult to resist. And so by relentlessly attacking our specialness as a nation, the Conservatives have quite literally been attacking our ability to survive as a nation at all.

The Man Who Misunderstood Canada

"WHAT DO YOU SUPPOSE," mused a prominent Canadian recently, "is going through his mind? What can Mulroney possibly be thinking of?"

It's a fair question to ask regarding a prime minister who systematically dismantles our social support, transportation and cultural networks; who signs away our autonomous ability to shape our own future and devastates our economy; who deliberately unleashes the separatist furies in Quebec; who sets region against region and Canadian against Canadian; who makes a career of weakening the national government at every turn.

Psychoanalysing public figures from a distance is a perilous business at best, and in this instance quite unnecessary. Much of Mulroney's motivation can readily be deduced from his own well-documented track record.

That motivation appears to stem not so much from vision, however misguided, as from profound shallowness. It is probably fair to say that Mulroney did not set out to wreck Canada. That prospect is merely the natural outcome of the course chosen by a leader who neither understands nor values this country sufficiently, who is bereft of fundamental philosophical principles to guide him, who is politically cunning but not intellectually thoughtful and who is driven more by ego than by foresight.

From earliest childhood, Brian Mulroney seems to have grown up with the idea that the United States is the big league, and Canada is just the farm team. The influences that helped shape him in this direction have been well documented in a succession of biographies. His native Baie-Comeau was a company town that owed its whole existence to clear-cutting the forest to meet the newsprint needs of a powerful American — Colonel Robert McCormick, who owned the *Chicago Tribune* and the *New York Daily News*. All his life, Mulroney himself has told with great relish how from the age of seven he had sung for the colonel whenever the great man visited the town, and had been rewarded each time with a U.S. $50 bill.

Later, when the adult Mulroney made the transition from labour-relations lawyer to corporate executive, it was as president of Iron Ore Company of Canada — the Canadian branch plant of a U.S. corporation. Once again he "sang" for his American superiors, by carrying out their mandate to execute a massive layoff of Canadian workers that included shutting down the entire mining town of Schefferville. This time, his reward was not a $50 bill, but financial security for life. And then, as prime minister, he literally sang for the president of the United States, crooning "When Irish Eyes Are Smiling" to an amiably grinning Ronald Reagan at the Shamrock Summit of 1985.

Mulroney's style throughout his years in office has consistently suggested a severe case of White House envy. For more than a year, Mulroney insisted on speaking from behind a massive presidential style lectern, complete with Canadian coat of arms, that was shipped around the country for his appearances. The first time the lectern was used, Mulroney even had himself introduced, presidential style, by a press aide: "Ladies and gentlemen, the Prime Minister." The immediate derision from the media was such that Mulroney never tried that introduction again, but the lectern remained a fixture for a year and a half. Other presidential trappings endure to this day in Mulroney's fondness for multicar motorcades and Secret Service–style phalanxes of security men.

Such imitativeness in our prime minister would be unattractive, but relatively harmless, of itself. But it is symptomatic of a far more serious, and deeply harmful, mirroring of the United States in matters of substance. Mulroney's statements and actions reflect a consistent belief that the Americans are the ones who know how to do things right — in economic management, in social policy, in their view of the world — and Canada will be a better country the more we emulate them in all respects. There is also, in both the style and the substance of his dealings with Presidents Reagan and Bush, an eagerness to please that borders on the obsequious. His handling of everything from the free-trade deal to foreign policy vividly brings to mind the image of a branch plant manager who regards the wishes, whether expressed or anticipated, of head office as beyond question.

The converse of this, of course, is that Mulroney has never shown any sign of understanding his *own* country, let alone appreciating the values and characteristics that make Canada distinctive and special. He is incapable of the leadership function of articulating for Canadians what is special about Canada, because he shows no sign of believing that Canada *is* all that special. The Canadian way of doing things seems to make him more impatient than appreciative. There is something close to contempt, for instance, in the way he spoke of the Canadian public's legitimate concerns about free trade in 1985: "Put an ideal like that, and you count on the country to come down squarely on both sides of the issue . . . A trade enhancement program of any kind in Canada would probably meet with an overwhelming degree of ambivalence. You would get six and you would lose half a dozen, in typical Canadian fashion."

To a leader who shows so little evidence of genuine pride in Canada himself, the notion that he might be "selling out" the nation through his trade deal or betraying Canadian values through his social cutbacks or destructive constitutional proposals would probably be incomprehensible. He simply appears not to operate from premises that would provide a basis for dedication to preserving any given aspect of Canadian life.

If his admiration for the American way provides one element of explaining Mulroney's performance in office, the fact that he entered politics without any strong political philosophy is another. All accounts of Mulroney's life prior to winning the Tory leadership in 1983 depict a man more concerned with personal achievement, success and power than with the pursuit of any substantive political agenda. The impression is of someone who wanted to become prime minister because it was the top job in the country, rather than because he wanted to lead the country in any particular direction. In his first run for the leadership, in 1976, he had positioned himself as a "Red Tory," on the party's left wing. In his successful 1983 bid, he courted the party's right-wingers who were disgruntled with then-leader Joe Clark's relative moderation. As Opposition leader, he presented himself to Canadians as a small-l liberal squarely in the political mainstream.

In fact, during a meeting with the editorial board of the *Toronto Star* shortly before the 1984 election, Mulroney sounded so Trudeau-like in his views that he was asked why he was a Tory rather than a Liberal. He replied that he might indeed have become a Liberal but for happenstance. There had been an active Progressive Conservative club at St. Francis Xavier University during his student days, but not a Liberal one, and things had just gone on from there.

Whether his political views genuinely swung back and forth, or whether he simply was whatever he thought influential people wanted him to be at any given moment, ideology clearly didn't play a big role in Mulroney's make-up. In fact, asked shortly before the 1983 leadership convention about ideological swings in his stance, Mulroney is reported to have replied: "Maybe that concern with ideology is why we have been in opposition so long."

It is probably fair to say that when Mulroney became prime minister he was an ideologically empty vessel, waiting to be filled by whatever political currents flowed most strongly toward him. Given Mulroney's own character and the circumstances of the time, it is scarcely surprising that he was soon swept away by the influences of the doctrinaire right. Every biography of Mulroney emphasizes his overwhelming desire to be liked and accepted, especially by the most powerful. With Ronald Reagan as president of the United States and Margaret Thatcher as prime minister of Britain, it is scarcely surprising that these two ultraconservatives

quickly became his role models. Becoming accepted into
the club of heavy-hitters, as Mulroney would have perceived it, required embracing Reaganism and Thatcherism
— two very similar approaches dedicated to minimizing
the role of government, virtually deifying business
decision-making as the source of all good, and leaving
the governance of society as much as possible to market
forces. He appears to have been influenced particularly
by Reagan's dogmatically ideological approach to issues,
and by Thatcher's success in proceeding with steely
determination to impose policies opposed by much of
the public. It is interesting to speculate what Mulroney's
policy course might have been, had there been instead a
Democrat in the White House and a Labour party
prime minister at 10 Downing Street.

Other forces undoubtedly converged with, and reinforced, the influence of Reagan and Thatcher in pushing Mulroney in a direction away from the Canadian
political mainstream. Having courted the right-wingers
in his party to undermine the hapless Joe Clark and win
the leadership, the new prime minister predictably
came under pressure from them to deliver on their
agenda of privatization, deregulation and program slashing. Having courted Quebec separatists to rebuild his
party in the province and having brought a number of
them into his cabinet and caucus, Mulroney equally
predictably came under pressure from them to deliver
on weakening the national government.

What ultimately cemented the shift of Mulroney and his
Tories to the right was the powerful new alliance between
this government and big business. Corporate leaders were
initially skeptical that Mulroney's actions did not go sufficiently far in matching his post-election conservative

rhetoric. But they increasingly came to recognize that this was a federal government far more open to their agenda than were any of its predecessors. That recognition dramatically changed the balance of political forces in Canada.

The federal Liberals had for decades been the party with the closest links to big business, for the simple reason that the Liberals had long been the main governing party. Business leaders saw little benefit in primarily allying themselves, financially or otherwise, with Conservatives who traditionally were relegated to Opposition with only periodic brief stints in government. The relationship between the business community and the Liberals had been a reasonably balanced one. Business did have influence on Liberal policy, but it never succeeded in dictating the agenda. At some times, on some issues, Liberal governments listened closely to business voices. Other times, as with the creation of the Foreign Investment Review Agency, Liberal policies infuriated multinational-dominated big business. For the most part, the business community accepted this sort of win-some, lose-some relationship as a fact of life.

Before the 1988 election, business leaders had come to realize that the relationship with the Mulroney Tories could be on an entirely different scale. This was a government increasingly prepared to follow a Reaganite, Thatcherite agenda that would leave the corporate sector ever more free to do whatever it pleased. This was a government whose electoral survival was worth going to almost any lengths to secure. And business did go to extraordinary lengths in the 1988 election, effectively buying victory for the Tories by burying the opposition parties in a multimillion-dollar avalanche of pro–free trade advocacy advertising with which they could not compete.

The election outcome sealed an unprecedented working alliance between our national government and a single powerful interest group, to the virtual exclusion of other voices in our society. Having gone to such spectacular lengths to help keep the Tories in power, business leaders predictably wanted them to reciprocate by following above all else the business blueprint for Canada's future. Mulroney, ever one to curry the favour of the powerful, had been shown just how potently helpful big business could be to his government if he continued to win its approval. This combination of developments has come to dictate the entire character of the Mulroney government, and begun to transform the very nature of Canada.

A more thoughtful leader might have been deterred by the dangers posed to the broad national interest by such a narrow alliance. But thoughtfulness and foresight have never been Mulroney's strong suit. He has always been much more a practitioner of the personally expedient. His pattern has been that of a man who hates to lose, and who therefore will pursue the "win" — the attainment of his personal objectives in a given situation — with little regard for broader consequences. The lesson of his years as a labour-relations lawyer representing management appears to have been that you always have to get a deal, no matter what — that's the "win." Any deal is better than no deal. If it's a less favourable deal than your clients would have wished, they can always recoup their losses in the next round of negotiations.

That kind of short-term orientation may work in the corporate sector, but in the complexities of government decision-making that affects the whole future of a country, it is disastrously short-sighted. Yet this belief that a "win" must always be achieved no matter what the cost, rather than thoughtful analysis of implications for the future, helps explain the pattern of Mulroney's approach to government.

He accepted the free trade deal with the United States over the advice of his own chief negotiator, who warned that the stated objective of secure access to the U.S. market had not been attained. He presided over the Meech Lake constitutional negotiations by simply giving each premier whatever was asked for, and sometimes concessions not even requested, rather than risk not getting a deal by speaking for the interests of the national government and Canada as a whole. He rammed the much-hated GST through a recalcitrant Senate by taking the unprecedented step of stacking the Senate with hastily-appointed extra Tory members, without regard to the public cynicism this would cause. It is thus entirely within the pattern of this let's-make-a-deal approach that Mulroney would have reflected little on the consequences for Canada of his de facto deal with the corporate community to dedicate his government to exclusive pursuit of its agenda.

Despite the dominant role Mulroney has played in charting the course of his government, and all the responsibility he must bear as leader, it would still be a mistake to overly demonize Mulroney as the *sole* author of our misfortunes. If he were to resign and be replaced by any other member of his cabinet, the Tory government would still be infected with the same mind-set that has inflicted all this damage on Canada.

In our parliamentary system, no prime minister can long impose his or her will single-handedly on an unwilling cabinet and caucus. There have been no cabinet revolts, no caucus uprisings, over the doctrinaire right-wing agenda during Mulroney's time in office. All his colleagues, and indeed his party as a whole, have freely chosen to accept his policies and directions rather than resign in protest. All his ministers, and hence all his potential successors, have advocated, implemented and defended the government's nation-wrecking policy initiatives and omissions. None can escape shared responsibility, nor be relied on to break decisively away from the orientation whose consequences we are all suffering. It would be a mistake to think that a new face as Tory leader would change the agenda that has become a firmly entrenched mind-set in the Tory party.

EIGHT

A Nation
Imperilled

I N EACH OF THE AREAS to which Mulroney and
his Tories have applied their reverse Midas
touch — social policy, the economy, culture,
transportation, free trade, the Constitution — the direct
devastation has been enormous. But what is even more
destructive is that the whole of the damage is greater
than the sum of its parts.

As a result of what they have done to various individual aspects of our national life, the Tories have wounded
something even more fundamental that goes to the very
essence of Canada and being Canadian — our national
psyche. They have altered our perception of ourselves,
eroded our confidence and shattered our hopes for the
future. That, in turn, has led to a breakdown of national
unity and, indeed, of certainty that Canada as we know
it is worth preserving.

It may seem hard to believe that cuts in a number of
programs, however important, a bad trade deal and
botched constitutional negotiations could have so crippling an effect in so short a time. But just as different
chemicals that individually are only mildly toxic can be

combined into an instantly lethal brew, it is the combined psychological effect of the Mulroney government's measures that is so poisonous.

The Tories have undermined our trust in government, in each other and ultimately in ourselves. At the same time, they have begun to wrest away from us the national "monuments" that are the touchstones of our identity.

Canadians as a society have historically placed a great deal of trust in our governments. The whole evolution of our system has been based on accepting, in fact demanding, a high degree of government involvement in shaping our national development. In doing this, we have regarded government not as some alien force but as our agent, the instrument of our collective will. We have taken it as a given that the government's mandate requires it to act within the parameters of our shared values. And we have taken it for granted that the government would give us the time and the opportunity to participate fully in any major decisions affecting our future.

We have thus felt able to assume, throughout our history, that the government of the day would seek to act in our best interests. If a given government failed to do so to our satisfaction, we would replace it with another. We would feel able to attribute its failure to incompetence or misguided priorities, certainly not to some attempt to impose a harmful and foreign agenda on the Canadian people against our will. Although confidence in a given party's government might wane, trust in our system of government remained intact.

Since 1984, however, all this has suddenly changed. The Mulroney government has been acting not as our agent, but as our master. There was never any expression of a collective Canadian wish to slash social programs, to undermine medicare, to devastate our economy with high interest rates and an over-valued dollar, to dismantle our railways, to cripple the CBC, to seek a free trade deal with the United States or to dismember our national government through constitutional change. Mulroney simply told us all these things *had* to happen, whether we liked it or not — and they had to happen *fast*, on his timetable. Then his government charged ahead with implementing them, over widespread public opposition.

For the first time in history, Canadians have come to feel helpless in the face of their own government. Suddenly it feels that our government is no longer on our side. It is doing things *to* us, not *for* us. We see changes happening that we know are harmful to ourselves and our country, and we are powerless to prevent them. In such a situation, people naturally turn inward. Unable to express their will through the national government, indeed feeling threatened by it, they turn increasingly to their provincial governments. They identify themselves ever more as Albertans, Quebecers, British Columbians, Nova Scotians and so on rather than as Canadians, seeking in these smaller units of identity a sense of control and a voice. The Mulroney government has been adding further momentum to this trend by transferring more and more jurisdiction and financial responsibility for programs to the provinces. This leads to a fragmentation not only in programs but in attitudes, with each province being driven increasingly to look out for its own interests instead of taking a more balanced and cooperative national approach.

These centrifugal tendencies would be destructive of national unity in themselves. At the same time, however, the provincial governments are suffering the impact of Mulroney's cutbacks in federal transfer payments, combined with tax revenue shortfalls resulting from the recession induced by Tory economic policies. Instead of being able to meet the needs and expectations of the citizens who have effectively given up on Ottawa, provincial governments — regardless of their political orientation — become forced to behave scarcely better than the Mulroney team. They find themselves with little financial choice but to slash their own programs and services as well. Everything from hospitals, to universities, to public transit, to welfare, becomes underfunded.

People find themselves paying more and more taxes for less and less service, and become increasingly disillusioned with all governments in general. This leads to more fragmentation still. Many people are turning in disgust and frustration to regional protest parties — the Reform party in the West, the Bloc Québécois in Quebec — that base their appeal on alienation, resentment and the most divisive us-against-them attitudes. Still others are losing hope and interest altogether, saying in effect: "To hell with the country, to hell with the government. All I care about is feeding my family, paying my mortgage and looking out for my own backyard. It doesn't matter to me anymore whether I'm Canadian or American, what political party is in power, whether Quebec goes or stays — it's become every man for himself."

The effects of loss of faith in government might have been mitigated by a continuing strong belief among Canadians in the ideal of Canada itself. But the actions of the Mulroney government have simultaneously eroded the roots of that belief by throwing into question our sense of national identity. Every country has its national monuments — focal points that come to attain enormous emo-

tional importance as unifying symbols of pride in its history
and its special attributes. The United States, for instance,
has its Statue of Liberty, its Grand Canyon, its Washington,
Jefferson and Lincoln memorials, and so on. Canada is perhaps unique, however, in that our real national "monuments" are neither statues nor places. Our monuments are
our social programs, our railways, our CBC.

These intrinsic parts of our nation's daily life have
over the years attained enormous emotional importance.
They have come to express our heritage, our identity
and our national pride. Even people who perceive little
financial stake in social programs, who never ride a train,
who seldom listen to the CBC, have a passionate attachment to these quintessentially Canadian institutions and
feel personally diminished by the spectacle of their dismantling. And small wonder. Our social programs, especially medicare, are an expression of our deeply ingrained,
distinctly Canadian vision of ourselves as a society that
takes care of its own, a "kinder, gentler" nation than our
neighbour to the south. Our national railway is the basic
economic institution of our history, the thread that
stitched the provinces together and made Canada possible. It is the elemental symbol of Canadian unity. And
the CBC is its spiritual partner. As the railway has linked
us through the movement of people and goods, the CBC
has linked us through the flow of ideas, music and enter-
tainment from coast to coast. The CBC is the living
expression of our commitment to nurturing a distinctive
Canadian culture and identity.

When our national government sets out to demolish
these institutions, there is no less an emotional impact
on Canadians than there would be on Americans if their
government were to blow up the Statue of Liberty, pave

over the Grand Canyon and tear down the Washington
Monument. In fact, the loss for us is vastly greater,
because we are a much younger country whose sense of
identity is still developing.

To attack these elements of our societal structure is to
undermine our sense of who we are. They are the very
cornerstones, the foundations of our identity, the key
symbols that help shore us up and hold us together.
Their gradual loss, along with other erosions of our
national fabric, leaves Canadians dispirited and confused.

If we are not the socially caring nation Canadians
used to know, what nation are we? If the railway is not
the symbol of our unifying history, what symbol can we
have? If the CBC is not to be our national voice, what
is? If we are not to be free to shape our own destiny as a
result of free trade, what kind of destiny can we antici-
pate? If our national government is to be constitutionally weakened to the point where it can no longer speak
for all Canadians, who will speak for us?

Unanswered questions of this magnitude cannot help
but begin dissolving the glue of shared purpose that
holds us together as a nation. If we cease knowing what
Canada means — if home no longer feels like home —
we lose the frame of reference for distinguishing between
positive proposals and yet more threats to our viability as
a nation. That, in turn, exposes us to the risks crystallized
in the old malapropism, "If you don't know where you're
going, you're liable to end up someplace else."

That is precisely the danger facing Canada if we continue on the present course. The more dispirited and
confused Canadians become, the easier it is to slip into
believing that further steps in the same direction are
either inevitable or scarcely matter anymore. Canadians

could, in the worst-case scenario, be seduced into giving the Tories enough additional time in power to carry their policies through to their logical conclusion. That may seem implausible, given how low the party has fallen in public esteem. But, based on Mulroney's record so far, the potential capacity of this team to hoodwink us yet again is not to be underestimated.

One scenario is that, as the next election draws closer, Mulroney might again slip into the guise of a compassionate progressive. A small tax cut here, a slight ratcheting down of interest rates there, a bit of new social spending thrown in too — some kind of child-care initiative, perhaps? — and Mulroney might claim that had been the plan all along. All the belt-tightening, program-slashing and extra-taxing had merely been necessary interim adjustments for pursuing the "sacred trust" of Canadian values ever more diligently. Of course, what would happen *after* the election can be inferred from what happened after the last two, when Mulroney each time immediately shifted gears and raced ahead with a right-wing agenda. But particularly if the major opposition parties fail to impress the voters, memories might be short enough to let him get away with it again.

A second scenario is that Mulroney might again pull his old trick of creating a crisis, and then insist that we have no choice but to follow his lead, or disaster is sure to ensue. He might conceivably try to do it again on the free trade issue, this time insisting we must accept free trade as well with Mexico, or somehow be engulfed by the spectre of terrible economic consequences. Or, more likely, he might attempt it on the issue of national unity, stage-managing a succession of events to let him argue that he needs a resounding electoral endorsement of his latest constitutional confection or Quebec will separate. He might, in fact, use both scenarios, combining a gentler, kinder Mulroney with a supposed choice between this version of himself and economic collapse or the break-up of Canada.

The third scenario for a great national hoodwinking is that Mulroney might step aside, to be replaced by someone like Joe Clark or Don Mazankowski. To the extent that people allowed their loathing of the man to mislead them into believing that Mulroney is all that is wrong with this government, such a leadership switch might be electorally effective. But the reality, of course, is that every potential successor within the cabinet has bought into and advanced the Tory agenda whose consequences we are suffering. A leadership change would give us a different salesman, perhaps a modified style of sales pitch, but the same devastatingly defective product.

And, finally, there is the Reform party scenario. To vote for this simplistic right-wing protest party would be to accept most of the Mulroney government's key philosophical premises — about reducing the role government can play on our behalf, wrecking the social safety net and becoming a meaner society. Even more than voting for the Tories, voting for this party which appeals to our fear and anger with policies even more regressive than those of the Tories. would be to reject the Canadian values that have sustained us throughout our history.

Moreover, strong voter support for Reform would be a likely way to ensure that the Tories return to power. Coupled with the electoral strength of the Bloc Québécois in Quebec, the election of a significant number of Reform members would create a thoroughly splintered minority Parliament. If the Reform party ended up with the balance of power to determine who formed the next government, it is most unlikely they would be ideologically comfortable with supporting the Liberals or the New Democratic Party. The closest compatibility would be with the Tories, whom they would likely end up maintaining in power on the basis of who knows what backroom deals to push the government even further to the right.

If the Tories do manage somehow to win enough additional time in power to carry their policies through to their logical conclusion, there will be nothing recognizably Canadian left about Canada. In fact, the risk is that our country will be altered beyond having any reason for existing as a nation at all.

Mulroney will turn out to have been all too candid with Canadians when he said shortly after the 1984 election: "Give us twenty years, and it is coming, and you will not recognize this country." Only it will not take 20 years. Just five more years of Tory government — five years of continuing, rather than reversing, what the Conservatives have already set in motion — will suffice to leave Canada not only unrecognizable as its former distinctive, free and thriving self, but probably non-viable. The prospect of the Tories' Canada five years from now is not a pretty picture.

We will have massive and chronic unemployment as a result of the combined effects of free trade; rising personal taxes that siphon spending money out of the economy; lack of major job creation and worker retraining initiatives; and a Bank of Canada mandated only to fight inflation with its interest rate policies. Workers increasingly desperate for jobs will be forced to accept downwardly spiralling wages and deteriorating work conditions. And the growing numbers who cannot find adequately paid work at all will lead to a rise in the number of homeless, to increased crime and to growing racial intolerance.

The destruction of the social safety net will greatly exacerbate all these problems. Diminishing support from unemployment insurance, welfare and other programs will leave the unemployed and the working poor with nowhere to turn. They will be pushed further to the margins of society. The most severely victimized by this will be the children, who will be denied opportunities and find themselves trapped in a generational cycle of poverty.

Medicare will collapse. The combination of dwindling federal cash transfers to provinces and a disappearing federal role in setting standards will lead to the end of our nationwide, payment-free system of health care. It will be replaced by a patchwork of different provincial systems, with steadily growing recourse to extra-billing and user fees readily affordable only to the well off, as well as rationing of health care to cut costs to government. Eventually, we will end up with a system like the one in the United States, where Medicare is available only to some of the poor and the quality and promptness of care everyone else gets depend on what he or she can afford to buy.

Policy making by the federal government will increasingly be abdicated to "market forces," in the form of an oligarchy of some 200 of the largest corporations, many of them foreign owned. Instead of a government that works in partnership with business and organized labour, we will have a government that makes itself ever more the *servant* of one powerful interest group. Instead of our democratic right to have elected officials act on our behalf, in our best interests, the policy agenda will increasingly be dictated solely by the profit motive of the biggest businesses.

Balkanization of the provinces will gather momentum. Constitutional changes along the lines already proposed by the Tories will transfer more powers to provincial governments and further weaken our already decentralized federal government. With a national government unwilling and increasingly unable to ensure that the broad national interest of all Canadians prevails over narrower regional and provincial claims, each province will be driven to look out just for itself. The quality of life of Canadians in the poorer provinces will diminish, as the richest provinces strive to keep more of their wealth for themselves instead of participating in redistribution as in the past. Resentments among regions will grow. And, in the absence of national leadership, provinces will compete with one another to attract new business investment by lowering standards in such areas as the environment and worker protection, to the detriment of the Canadian people.

Lack of national cohesion and federal support will paralyse our economic development. Regional development programs, regarded by the Americans as unfair trade subsidies, will be phased out. Canadian research and development, already grossly underfunded by the Tories, will continue to be starved for cash, crippling our ability to produce innovations that would enhance our competitiveness in a changing world. High-tech education, post-secondary schooling and retraining will likewise continue getting short shrift, leaving our human resources to atrophy.

Quebec will separate by degrees. The Tories will proceed with constitutional policies designed to let Quebecers be as separate from the rest of Canada as possible while staying nominally within Confederation. The more economically and politically autonomous Quebec becomes, the more irrelevant being part of Canada will seem to Quebecers. Quebec will withdraw further and further into itself, until eventually the link with Canada will seem like an atrophied vestige that might as well be severed.

Free trade with Mexico will strike a final blow to our ability to manage our own economy. We will be locked into a continental integration that will, in effect, gradually recolonialize us. The United States will get most of the powerful and lucrative decision-making, product development, financial and other high-order service sector jobs. Mexico will supply the cheap labour at what would be starvation wages for Canadian workers. And we will be relegated to selling off our natural resources at ever-diminishing prices — unless the American multinationals can buy them even cheaper elsewhere — until all we have left to peddle is our water. We will, quite literally, be reduced to hewers of wood and drawers of water.

None of this needs to happen. What the Tories have already done to Canada is wide-ranging, deeply damaging and painful — but none of it is irreversible. Another five years of the Tory agenda, however, and we will be far past the point of no return. Too much will have been dismantled, too much of our independence will have been surrendered, too many of the ties that bind us together will have been severed, for there to be any realistic chance of regaining what will have been lost. Bereft of our sense of identity, our confidence in our abilities, our hope for the future, we will have squandered the Canada that is the birthright of our children.

Right now we still have a choice. We still have the option of pursuing a very different, far more positive vision of Canada's future.

NINE

Empires of the Mind

WE NEED, AS CANADIANS, to recognize once again that anything is possible for Canada. Far from being forced by the circumstances of a changing world to gradually disintegrate, our nation has the potential — perhaps more than any other country on earth — to capitalize on those circumstances and build a future even better than our past.

Just as our riches in natural resources enabled us to grow strong and prosperous in the resource-hungry world of the past, so too we are rich in other potential advantages that can enable us to thrive in the emerging global economy of tomorrow. That is why there is an alternative vision of Canada's future that reflects true Canadian values, acknowledges our advantages, stimulates our innovative capabilities, inspires faith and rekindles our commitment to growing ever more prosperous, progressive and dynamic.

It is a vision that recognizes the inextricable link between the creation of wealth and the sharing of it, between successful economic policy and supportive social policy, between building our prosperity and strengthening our distinctive Canadian identity. And it is a vision that understands the phenomenon of globalization not as a wave that must wash away everything we have cherished about Canada, but as a powerful current that we can ride to new national achievements.

Some people would have us believe that globalization is an inescapable fact of life that requires us to abandon much that we hold dear, and that we have no choice but to bow to all its dictates. Others insist that globalization is just a buzzword concocted by big business to con us into doing whatever the corporations want. In fact, both positions are wrong. Globalization is a fact of life — but we *do* very much have a choice about how we respond to its challenges.

There is no doubt we are in a new world economy that is global in scope. The dynamics of trade have been dramatically altered by advances in transportation, telecommunications and computerization, by vastly accelerated movements of capital, by the lowering of trade barriers and by the emergence of Third World countries as major sources of production. Corporations can now operate as if national borders and even geography scarcely exist, buying raw materials wherever they find the best price, employing labour wherever it is cheapest, borrowing money wherever they get the lowest interest rates and investing wherever they get the best return. Then they can ship their products — and sometimes, through telecommunications, even their services — to wherever there are sufficient concentrations of customers. The locations where resources are purchased and where production is carried out can be changed with almost blinding speed in response to shifting market conditions.

This new flexibility enables multinational corporations to hold governments to ransom, playing off one country against another with the threat of being bypassed as a site for corporate investments. We are told that if we're too tough with our environmental standards, business can go to Mexico, where there are scarcely any standards at all. If our worker salaries are too high, production will be transferred to Tennessee, where people work in non-unionized sweatshops for a fraction of the cost. But the Tennesseeans, in turn, are told that unless they drop their wages lower still, production can always be shifted to some Asian country where people are willing to work seven days a week for even less money. This concept of globalization is, in short, a formula for surrendering the decision-making powers of the state to the multinational corporations. Unless we do exactly what they want — and what they want is to call the shots in accordance with their profit motive, with a minimum of interference from government — they will go somewhere else that's more amenable.

For a country like Canada, to accept this approach to global competitiveness is to get caught in a game we have no hope of winning. However far we lower our environmental standards, there will always be some country willing to despoil its environment even more drastically to generate short-term wealth. However much we lower worker health and safety standards, there will always be some other country where human life counts for even less. However far we reduce salaries and chop social programs, there will always be some other country where impoverished workers have no choice but to toil in even meaner conditions. This way of dealing with global competition is a trap that could make sweatshops

of the future out of entire economically advanced countries of today.

If we play this game, we will eventually see our environment ravaged, our resources depleted at fire-sale
prices, our standard of living plummeting ever downward. Thus transformed, we will have lost forever our
capacity to make hopeful choices for the future. And
then, wrung dry, we will still be cast aside by the multinationals in favour of some other location that offers
even cheaper and more favourable conditions.

But now we still have a choice. We can choose not to
play this particular game, in which we would be doomed
to certain eventual defeat and economic and social devastation. We can choose instead to compete in a very
different game, one that plays to our strengths rather
than our weaknesses: the game of competing through
the brainpower, creativity and knowledge of Canadians.

Canada, like every other economically advanced
country including the United States, can no longer
count on being able to maintain any competitive advantage against cheap-labour developing countries in the
mass manufacturing of standardized goods. Where we
do have the potential to compete effectively and to
thrive is in areas where the key to success is the application not of abundant cheap labour but of knowledge,
education, innovativeness and specialized skill.

We need to reorient our economy toward the types of
knowledge-intensive manufacturing activity where these
assets provide the greatest competitive benefit. We need
to focus increasingly on the production of specialized,
high-value-added goods that require a high degree of
adaptability, know-how and sophistication. And, perhaps
above all, we need to focus on innovation in the devel-

opment of new products and the improvement of existing ones. It is in these areas that, by virtue of more
advanced expertise and higher levels of education, we
can hope to prevail in competition with other countries
without having to write off our standard of living.

The world is moving in a direction where knowledge
itself has become a resource as real, meaningful and trad-
able as raw materials have been in the past. Knowledge
is in fact the best kind of resource, since it has the
invaluable quality of sustainable growth. Knowledge
cannot be depleted. By its very nature, it can only grow
and develop as knowledge breeds ever more knowledge.
That is why the new growth industries of knowledge-
intensive services and manufacturing know no bounds
and require only education, research and development
to forever renew themselves. As Winston Churchill once
declared with remarkable foresight: "The empires of the
future are empires of the mind."

Our choice is whether we group ourselves among the
advanced economies of the future by a major refocusing
of our economy in this direction, or condemn ourselves
to becoming part of the less-developed world by playing
the globalization game as defined by the multinationals
and the governing Tories. The global economy is gradually segmenting into two groups of countries: those affluent nations that carry out the high-value-added, knowledge-intensive activities of product development, design,
research, management and planning; and the comparatively impoverished rest of the world to which the actual
labour of production is farmed out.

Japan, for instance, started out in the second group,
using its hard-working and relatively ill-paid workers to
produce cheap copies of products developed in Western

countries. Now it has moved so far into the high-value-added group of countries that it is increasingly locating production offshore, and countries like Canada have been vying for the privilege of being the sites of Japanese car-assembly plants. Our choice is either to compete on the leading edge of innovation, specialization and other knowledge-based endeavours, or to be relegated to the role of a Third World production platform.

Few countries, in fact, are more ideally positioned than Canada to become world leaders in the new knowledge- and expertise-based global economy. In countries such as the United States, there is a clear pattern apparent in the types of locations that become centres of innovative, high-tech activity. Leading-edge industries gravitate to places that are near one or more high-quality universities, that have a well-educated work force and that are able to attract and keep the best experts by providing a safe, clean environment and a high standard of living and superior quality of life — places, in short, that closely resemble Canada as a whole.

It is a special blessing for Canada that those very qualities that best reflect Canadian values and of which Canadians have been proudest are precisely the attributes that are a key to success in the new era. Far from trying to make ourselves more like less fortunate countries, as the Tories and big business advocate, we should keep building on these formidable strengths we already have.

The degree of competitive advantage we can build on this foundation is limited only by the extent of our determination and the intensity of our efforts as a society. In the previous mass-manufacturing–dominated world economy, comparative advantage was static — a country either had advantages or it didn't — because it depended on geography and on such relatively unchangeable factors as access to raw materials, cheap labour and capital.

In the new knowledge-intensive global economy, comparative advantage is dynamic — that is, it can be created by appropriate strategies — because the emphasis is shifting from accidents of nature or demographics to the outputs of the human mind. As University of California professor Chalmers Johnson explained: "The newer dynamic concept of comparative advantage replaces the classical criteria with such elements as human creative power, foresight, a highly educated work force, organizational talent, the ability to choose, and the ability to adapt. Moreover, these attributes are not conceived of as natural endowments but as qualities achieved through public policies such as education, organized research and investment in social overhead capital."

The role of public policy, implemented by our national government on our behalf, is crucial. Canada has most of the necessary raw ingredients for thriving in this new arena of competition, but there's no way they add up to a recipe for success if we just sit back and passively wait for it to happen. Just like all our previous achievements in building Canada from a wilderness into one of the most successful nations in the world, rising to this new challenge and opportunity requires an act of our national will.

We must have the will to be pioneers of change in a rapidly changing world, the conviction that our future course is both desirable and feasible and the sound judgment to choose leadership that will set in motion the necessary economic and social policies to achieve our goal. We need a genuine national industrial strategy that identifies a limited number of knowledge-intensive, innovation-based sectors as key areas of opportunity for our future and then pours all the necessary effort into making us world leaders in those fields. Conservatives and big-business leaders sneer at the very mention of a national industrial strategy, regarding any such planning role by the state as foolish meddling with market forces. Yet Canada stands virtually alone among the economically advanced nations in lacking such a strategy.

The United States pursues industrial strategy in a variety of ways, most notably through massive targeted spending under the guise of national defence and the space program. The European Community has initiatives such as Esprit, the European Strategic Program on Information Technologies, a ten-year project jointly funded by business, government and universities to upgrade the competitiveness of member countries in micro-electronics, computer design and software. And Japan, of course, has its Ministry of International Trade and Industry, better known as MITI, which has played a leading hands-on role in guiding every aspect of that nation's emergence as a trade superpower.

Canada, on the other hand, has lagged farther and farther behind in research and development activities which go to the very heart of being competitive in the emerging innovation- and knowledge-based global economy. Of 23 countries in the Organization for Economic Co-operation and Development (OECD), Canada has plummeted in overall R & D effort from tenth place in 1984, when the Tories came to power, to 17th place in 1990, according to the World Economic Forum. Far from being consistent with the quest for competitiveness the Mulroney government keeps trumpeting, lack of massive government leadership and support in the field of research and development is a prescription for economic self-immolation.

Like virtually every other industrially advanced country in the world, we too need a strategy that says here are the things we can be good at, here is where we can be innovative and competitive, here is where we can most usefully concentrate enough of our financial resources to accomplish something, here is what we have to be researching and developing, here is the corporate and academic behaviour we should be encouraging. That way, we can identify a few areas where we have particular potential — be they the new ceramics, specialty steels, biotechnology, artificial intelligence, environmental technology or whatever else — recruit some of the very best people in those areas from around the world, and settle for nothing short of becoming world leaders.

This kind of strategic targeting offers the double benefit of being able to meet our own domestic requirements while at the same time developing leading-edge export industries. In a field like the environment, for instance, Canada needs to find more effective and cost-efficient new ways to clean up polluted lakes and rivers, to prevent acid rain and counteract its effects, to handle oil spills, to deal with the mountains of waste our society produces, to harvest our forests by methods that promote sustainable growth and to produce safer, cleaner alternative forms of energy. By committing the effort and resources to become pioneers in these fields, we can develop technologies that we can sell around the world and can establish ourselves as leaders in a new growth industry of the future.

We need, as well, to do a much better job of tapping the creativity and inventiveness of Canadians in every field. It happens far too often that someone in Canada invents a new product, technology or process that has great promise, but cannot find the financial, production and promotional support needed to bring the idea to market. The invention either dies for lack of support or ends up being developed and produced in another country to be sold back to us. In a world where new ideas are the key to prosperity, that is an absurd squandering of our potential.

Fulfilling that potential by encouraging and supporting innovation is an opportunity all the more readily available to a country like Canada, which already has a successful history of direct government involvement in so many aspects of our development. "Market forces" alone, in a comparatively small economy with an exceptionally high degree of foreign ownership of corporations, cannot realistically be expected to provide an environment for individual innovators that is any more hospitable in the future than it has been in the past. What we need to fill the gap is a government body, probably a new Crown corporation, to play the role of "Innovations Canada."

This body would actively encourage people with creative new ideas to come forward. It would identify the most promising ones, provide development funding where needed, work vigorously to create link-ups between these innovators and Canadian companies to produce what they have invented and publicize Canadian innovations to facilitate their marketing. This new body could also act as a clearing house and directory for innovation, allowing people at work on similar ideas in different parts of the country an opportunity to find out about one another and perhaps attain synergy and cost efficiencies by pooling their efforts. The combined effect of such measures, carried out in a high-profile manner, would be to build a steadily growing momentum for innovation as an accumulation of success stories inspired more and more creative Canadians to believe in their own ideas and explore their potential.

Focusing on knowledge- and innovation-based industrial growth does not mean writing off all our existing, traditional industries. But since global competition in wages and prices for mass production is a game few Canadian companies can win in the long run, we must help as many firms as possible adapt so that they can compete in areas of potential strength. Such adaptations include targeting markets for high-end products where quality is a bigger factor than price, specialization into market niches, customizing products and emphasizing product innovation. Like building a world role in leading-edge industries, reorienting our traditional industries can be achieved on a sufficient scale only if we have a coherent industrial strategy and effective leadership and support from the national government.

Canada's opportunities in the new knowledge-intensive global economy may be even greater in the service sector. As one of still relatively few "post-industrial" societies in a world predominantly composed of newly industrializing countries, we should be able to become leaders in the large and growing global export market for knowledge and expertise. Canadian service firms are already powerful international competitors in such fields as banking, life insurance, consulting engineering and real estate development. But we have barely begun to tap the export potential — in both the private sector and government — of Canadian expertise in a broad variety of other activities that we have not until now recognized as exportable products.

By far the most promising market for increased export of our services is in those same newly industrializing countries with which we cannot effectively compete in mass-production manufacturing. Their economies are growing and becoming more complex. Their populations are migrating to urban centres to work in factories. They are, in short, experiencing an industrial revolution that urgently requires them to build up and modernize their infrastructures. Yet these countries typically have a shortage of experienced technical managers and expertise, both in the private sector and in government. This weakness tends to be particularly acute in the public sector, where civil servants lack the experience to plan the best use of natural resources and to meet the new demands on government that come with rapid economic growth and urbanization. With the revenues that come from their manufacturing successes based on cheap and hard-working labour, more and more of these countries can afford to import the specialized skills, information and knowledge they need from industrially advanced nations like Canada.

We, in turn, have the capacity to sell such countries state-of-the-art services in everything from waste management, road design and fire-fighting to urban transportation and health-care management. In a field like health care, for instance, Canada could offer governments of newly industrializing countries a highly innovative "turnkey" package that would include public-sector management and planning expertise; hospital and clinic construction; administration of health-care institutions; and medical, nursing and laboratory training.

While other economically advanced countries also have a stake in pursuing this growing services market, Canada has some unique competitive advantages that give us the edge if we have the foresight and the will to vigorously enter this field. Because Canada is neither a superpower nor a nation with any history of international colonialism, our involvement in the development of a country's infrastructure is likely to be more politically palatable to it. As well, we have more experience than many other industrialized nations in a direct government role in setting up and running programs and services, rather than following a more privatized model. Since most of the newly industrializing countries have a high degree of centralized government involvement in the economy and all aspects of development, the knowledge we can offer is more relevant to their approach than is that of most of our competitors.

The main benefit of becoming world leaders in the export of knowledge-intensive services would be the direct creation of wealth in the Canadian economy from foreign payments for those services. Since a sizeable share of the exports would be in the form of government-to-government deals, the resulting revenues — along with tax revenues generated by private-sector exports — would improve the federal government's financial position and increase its ability to afford other initiatives.

Service exports would also create jobs for Canadians. The number of new jobs directly created within Canada by any one deal would likely be limited. But the cumulative employment impact of all the *many* export opportunities available to us would be considerable — and such jobs tend to be high-quality and well-paying. As well, trade in services indirectly creates many additional jobs by giving us an advantage in selling related goods or other services to the countries involved. When the projects on which Canadian experts provide advice require the purchase of materials or equipment, it often makes sense for those advisors to recommend Canadian-manufactured products in which they already have confidence. That, in turn, creates new exports, jobs and revenues for Canada. Similarly, whenever we train or educate people from developing countries in Canada, we are in effect generating future export sales. As those students return home and become part of the decision-making business or government elite in their countries, it is Canadian expertise, products, approaches and companies that will be most familiar to them and that they will be most likely to use.

In our emphasis on knowledge-intensive services, we should not overlook our enormous untapped potential in the traditional service area of tourism. Fewer than 10 per cent of foreign visitors to Canada come from countries other than the United States. The Americans, in contrast, attract more than 30 per cent of their foreign tourists from overseas. That suggests we have not tapped the full potential of the European and Pacific Rim tourist markets.

Visitors who do come from overseas marvel particularly at our country's astounding natural beauty and relatively unspoiled environment. But their comparatively small numbers are evidence that we can generate a great deal more wealth and employment if we recognize the opportunity open to us. We need to devise more effective and better targeted marketing strategies and customized, environmentally sensitive guided tour packages that develop the tourism potential of our economically starved North.

In the service sector and manufacturing alike, being competitive in the world means *looking to the world* — not just to the United States. It makes no sense to talk, as Mulroney's Tories do, of globalization and then to focus virtually all our attention not on global trade but on a single neighbouring economy. Whatever Brian Mulroney may think, the United States alone is not the globe, and in fact it faces the same competitive challenges in a rapidly changing world as we do.

Coupled with the refocusing of our economy toward the types of activity in which we can have a bright future, there has to be a vigorous and sustained new drive by our national government to sell our products and services to the world. Instead of being mesmerized by the fact that the United States is currently our largest trading partner, we need to revitalize our rapidly atrophying trade links with the European Community, make a far more dynamic effort to prosper in the massive markets of the Pacific Rim and establish ourselves firmly in the future growth markets of Africa and the new Eastern Europe.

Globalization need not be our enemy; competitiveness need not be a formula for impoverishing our nation and our people. We do not need to fear what is happening in the world. If we view our situation in the clear light of good sense rather than through the distorting prism of doctrinaire right-wing ideology, we will see much to revitalize our hope for the future. With shared will and effective national leadership, we can harness both globalization and the new competitiveness as engines of our progress and prosperity.

There is every reason to believe we can succeed. It simply makes no sense to think that a country with as much going for it as Canada cannot find a way to be economically strong in today's and tomorrow's world.

TEN

The Educational Imperative

FOR CANADA TO COMPETE effectively in the new knowledge-intensive global economy, excellence in education is our single most important strategic weapon. It is no exaggeration, in fact, to say that education is as fundamentally vital an element of our basic economic framework in the new knowledge-oriented world as was the public infrastructure of roads, railways, ports and energy sources in the previous, predominantly mass-manufacturing era.

Our only alternative to self-destructively competing with other countries in having the cheapest workers is competing in having the *highest-quality* labour force. Nothing can stop us from being in the forefront of global competition in this regard if we develop enough world-class experts to provide innovation and leadership, as well as a general work force with the knowledge, skills, adaptability, ingenuity and motivation to carry out sophisticated and rapidly changing tasks. And for individual Canadians, having a suitable education will increasingly be the indispensable key to obtaining satisfying, well-paid employment and the confidence to participate vigorously in the global race for knowledge-based excellence.

Meeting the educational imperative is all the more urgent for Canada since other countries, notably including the United States, are already recognizing and beginning to respond to its decisive role in international competition. The U.S. National Commission on Excellence in Education, for instance, declared as long ago as 1983 in its much-publicized report, *A Nation at Risk*: "Knowledge, learning, information and skilled intelligence are the new raw materials of international commerce and are today spreading throughout the world as vigorously as miracle drugs, synthetic fertilizers and blue jeans did earlier. If only to keep and improve on the slim competitive edge we still retain in world markets, we must dedicate ourselves to the reform of our educational system for the benefit of all — old and young alike, affluent and poor, majority and minority. Learning is the indispensable investment required for success in the information age we are entering."

The Carnegie Forum on Education and the Economy pointed out in 1986: "In the future, high wage level societies will be those whose economies are based on the use of very highly skilled workers, backed up by the most advanced technologies available . . . America must now provide to the many the same quality of education presently reserved for the fortunate few. The cost of not doing so will be a steady erosion in the American standard of living."

But here in Canada, the Mulroney government has spent its years in office cutting back funding for universities, giving short shrift to training programs and at best muttering vaguely about the importance of education.

Eager as they have been to mirror American thinking in virtually every other area, Mulroney and his ministers ironically have lagged far behind in the one area where U.S. views correspond with what the most thoughtful Canadians have been saying for years.

Yet we in Canada have the potential for an enormous competitive advantage over the United States and many other countries in our ability to respond to the educational imperative, because we are starting from a much more favourable point of departure. We do not have the desperately underfunded, overcrowded schools and demoralized teachers that characterize so many U.S. cities. We have been spared the ghettos of generational poverty that squander human potential and undermine the likelihood of advancement in education in the United States. And we have avoided the class distinctions that in some European countries such as Britain steer young people into different qualities of education depending on their parents' background. Consequently, pursuing excellence in education does not require Canada to undertake the massive structural and attitudinal overhauls needed in some other countries.

Although we have this head start, however, we still have a very considerable distance to go toward attaining the scope and quality of education we need. Approximately one–third of all young Canadians today drop out before completing high school, while far too many of those who do graduate are nevertheless seriously deficient in the vital skills of reading, coherent writing and mathematics and sadly ignorant in such important subjects as science, history and geography.

It used to be the case that low levels of education or lack of specific skills did not preclude people from obtaining steady, reasonably well paid employment. In fact, it was not uncommon for bright, highly motivated people with very little formal education to start at the bottom and work their way up to senior positions, even to the presidency of a large corporation. But now the career ladder has been truncated. Young people who start at the bottom with inadequate education and few skills will at best face the prospect of staying at the bottom, in low-paid, dead-end jobs. More likely, they will increasingly become altogether unemployable, as those marginal jobs steadily disappear.

Low-skilled, low-paid jobs in manufacturing will be lost to newly industrializing countries with even lower rates of pay. At the same time, automated machinery is more and more capable of carrying out the routine tasks that have been the domain of the unskilled and uneducated — not only in factories but also in offices, banks, fast-food outlets and a vast range of other businesses. Combined with the shift of our economy toward knowledge-intensive service sector activities, these changes leave those without adequate education with scant hope of employability in as little as five to ten years. That, in turn, would result in personal hardship for the individuals involved, squandered human potential, soaring social support costs and forgone prosperity for our society as a whole.

It is not only competitiveness that requires Canada to ensure having a well-educated population. As the issues facing our society become ever more complex, the effective functioning of our democratic system of government depends on having a sufficiently knowledgeable citizenry to make informed political choices. Without that, we risk having huge numbers of Canadians tuning out all interest in politics and leaving decision making to a small elite of the well educated. Conversely, we could eventually have great numbers of the insufficiently informed falling under the influence of simplistic demagogues and steering our society in directions dictated by emotions of the moment rather than by knowledgeable judgment.

That is why we need, across Canada, an education system equal to the challenge of preparing young people not only for the work force but also, more generally, for life and for citizenship in the 21st century. The attributes of a genuinely literate person — a knowledge of history, geography, the arts, the sciences, politics, other cultures and so on — are even more essential in the complicated world of today and tomorrow than in the past.

The notion that we must choose between an education system dictated by the needs of the workplace or one that focuses on a more "liberal" education to prepare students for life in general is a widespread misconception. The reality is that today the business community and society at large converge remarkably closely in their needs from the education system. The kinds of jobs available in our society, and the actual content of various jobs, are changing so rapidly that to concentrate on providing students with specific vocational skills by the time they leave high school would be worse than useless. Most people who are in school now are likely to have at least two or three occupations in the course of their working lives. Within any given occupation, they will need to keep adapting and learning as new technologies and techniques come into effect. What the workplace needs most, consequently, is entrants with the broad foundation of fundamental knowledge, skills, ability to think for themselves and an ability to learn that

will enable them to adapt to new job-specific requirements in a constantly changing work environment.

Our primary and secondary school systems were initially developed with an eye to the prevailing needs of a
mass-manufacturing industrial workplace. The values
that were stressed included rote learning, discipline,
obedience to authority in a hierarchical structure and
the acquisition of basic skills. Then, beginning in the
1960s, the pendulum swung to the opposite extreme.
Educational thinking veered toward an emphasis on
abstract notions of individual self-fulfilment and self-
esteem. What a child learned was deemed to be far less
important than how the child *felt*. Children were to "discover" for themselves rather than be taught; they were
to learn at their own pace; choices proliferated and the
curriculum was overloaded. Any emphasis on pursuing
defined learning outcomes for each student was
shunned as repressively authoritarian. Now, in the
knowledge-intensive 1990s, we are beginning to recognize that an entire generation has gone through this system and emerged with degrees and diplomas but scarcely any fundamental education.

We need, as a society, to rediscover our sense of purpose about the educational enterprise. We need, not to
turn back the clock to earlier, outdated teaching methods,
but to move forward in recognition that the advances in
teaching techniques developed over the past decades
must be used to produce effective learning results. We
must affirm that a meaningful education does not merely entail keeping young people in schools for a pre-
scribed number of years. It has to entail the demonstrable acquisition of specific knowledge and specific skills.
Simply put, we must decide as a society what young

people should know and be able to do by the time they leave school to be equipped with the fundamentals to participate fully in an increasingly sophisticated workplace and in a complex society. And then we must make our education systems accountable for bringing all their students to the demonstrable acquisition of that knowledge and those skills. That requires rethinking all the current practices that work against this — including ability grouping, streaming, proliferation of subject choices, lack of standardized testing to monitor individual progress and insufficiency of individual help for students in difficulty.

Essential as it is to ensure that all our elementary and secondary school students learn what we as a society decide they need to learn, it would not suffice to stop there. We need as well to revitalize the capacity of our universities to play a leading role in the development of the knowledge-intensive society Canada must become to thrive in today's world. Canadian universities have to be capable of producing well-educated generalists and superbly trained specialists. Our universities should be world-class centres of innovation and creativity. And they should serve as magnets to attract clusters of sophisticated private-sector business seeking to draw on their expertise, research and resources. The ability of any given university to fulfil these roles depends largely on the resources at its disposal: the expertise, creativity and reputations of the professors it can afford to recruit; the ratio of faculty to students, which determines the degree of individual attention available; the quality of the facilities and equipment, especially libraries and research installations; and the availability of funding for research.

For virtually all Canadian universities, all these elements have been eroded in recent years by the Mulroney government's cutbacks in transfer payments to the provinces for post-secondary education, coupled with chronic underfunding by provincial governments. At a time when our system of post-secondary education is more important than ever to our development, it is absurd to allow our universities to lapse into stifling impoverishment and mediocrity. Financially starving our universities and other post-secondary institutions is a profoundly self-defeating false saving. We urgently need, instead, to recognize as a society that investing in excellence in education is an imperative condition of our future success in the global economy.

Learning in today's society has become of necessity a lifelong process. However solid a foundation of formal education we provide our young people, they will continually have to acquire and hone job-specific skills as they change occupations or as their work evolves. And most adults already in the work force face the necessity of constantly upgrading existing skills or learning new ones if they are to avoid being rendered obsolete by rapid changes in employment requirements.

In fact, "retraining" has become a buzzword among politicians and business leaders. But incessantly repeating that buzzword and tossing some money to a few retraining programs misses the point. It doesn't even begin to meet the needs of more than a million Canadians who are unemployed already, and of the many more who will be displaced as our economy continues its evolution.

It's all very well to agree that we need retraining. But retraining for *what*? To what occupations should currently unemployed workers be redirected? In what fields can we be sure there will actually be sufficient demand for their newly acquired skills once they are retrained? Which types of previous work experience best qualify people for retraining into which fields? What mechanisms can be established to provide all displaced workers with effective individual assessment and counselling to guide them toward the most appropriate new occupations? Who shares in the benefits of retraining? Who should carry it out? Who should pay for it? How do we make it all happen, quickly and efficiently, on a scale sufficient to meet the need and on an ongoing rather than a stopgap basis?

Such questions can be answered satisfactorily only by developing a cohesive and well thought out national retraining strategy that defines needs and opportunities, assigns roles and responsibilities for implementation, ensures the necessary funding, and establishes the structures through which all of this can be carried out.

From the earliest years of school through university to the upgrading and retraining of adult workers, every element of our education system must be seen not in isolation but as part of an integrated whole that will determine Canada's future as a nation. We cannot aspire to success, let alone leadership, in knowledge-intensive global competition unless we help every Canadian to become intensely knowledgeable.

A national industrial strategy cannot be developed in isolation from a national education strategy. Even though elementary and secondary education are constitutionally under exclusive provincial jurisdiction, it is time to recognize that we have a broader national interest in them. Our whole country has a stake in the education of every Canadian, because every Canadian will become either a contributor to the success of our economy or another statistic of failure that prevents us from achieving our goals. If we want to be recognized internationally as leaders in the quality of the education of our work force, that quality cannot vary from one province or territory to another. The global marketplace should be able to look at us and say, "*The Canadians* have the best educated and most innovative and highly skilled workers." It should not have to pick and choose only given areas of the country to regard favourably. And in a country where workers move from province to province, every province has a stake in the educational performance of every other province. That being the case, it would be pointless to pretend that our national stake in education begins only after high school, when the foundations of every young person's lifelong learning successes or failures have already been laid.

We therefore need to agree as a nation on the necessary goals and learning outcomes of every stage of the education process. That can happen only through direct involvement and leadership by our federal government in working with the provinces to develop a national strategy and national standards to meet the challenge of the educational imperative. With all these elements in place and with sufficient national will, there is nothing to stop Canadians from being the best educated people in the world. We cannot afford to settle for anything less.

ELEVEN

Hard-Hats to Babysitters

I F EVER THERE WAS A CASE where the dictates of enlightened self-interest and of basic human decency coincide, it must surely be in the need to intensify our pursuit of social justice for all Canadians.

In the new knowledge-intensive global competitiveness in which people are the most important resource, we will thrive only if we have not merely a well-educated but also a healthy and socially secure population. We cannot afford to squander human potential through grinding poverty, or through the distractions that arise when people lack social support.

But more than self-interest alone requires us to renew and revitalize our commitment to being a country that truly exists for the benefit of *all* its people. Even if it were possible for us to profit economically by relegating the less fortunate to the margins of society and closing our eyes to suffering that does not affect us directly, the price would be the loss of our soul and identity as a nation. We could not be such a society and still be the Canada most Canadians want, a Canada that can inspire the dedication and loyalty of its people through the quality of its values.

That, at root, is why we must take decisive action against the debasements of homeless people sleeping on sidewalk grates, of more than a million children going hungry and deprived, of the elderly lining up at food banks for sustenance, of women being brutalized and demeaned, of workers deprived of both employment and participation in society, of aboriginal Canadians still consigned to squalor and poverty after more than a century of injustice. We must rid ourselves of such affronts to elemental human dignity for the most compelling of all reasons — because they are *wrong*. If being Canadians is to mean anything, if being citizens of the world is to mean anything, we must reassert against all cynicism that for us it means a proud and fundamental commitment to dignity and social justice for every single member of our society.

The very first thing we need to do is stop the disintegration of medicare and of our social safety net that is resulting from Mulroney's cutbacks in programs and transfer payments. We cannot succeed in becoming world leaders by failing to remain Canadians. We cannot strengthen our economy by weakening our infrastructure. Only self-destruction could result from continuing the Mulroney government's policy of using deficit reduction as an excuse to dismantle precisely those instruments that offer the best hope of easing our transition into a progressive, knowledge-intensive, people-oriented society of the future.

But it is not enough merely to repair the damage inflicted by the Mulroney government. A powerful first step in moving forward would be to unequivocally affirm our commitment to meeting the basic human needs of all our citizens by entrenching it in our Constitution. If

Canadians agree that our sense of shared responsibility for one another's well-being is in our own enlightened self-interest and a defining element of our national identity, it is only sensible to give it expression in our most fundamental law which sets out the cardinal rules of our national existence. A judicially enforceable constitutional charter of social rights would prevent any future government from practising social Darwinism by ruthlessly throwing vulnerable Canadians to the mercy of "market forces." It would give the force of law to such elemental human rights as adequate food, housing, clothing, education, medicare and a safe environment.

Critics of such a charter argue that it would be risky to transfer some of the power in the field of social policy from legislatures to the courts. But risky for whom? Yes, the courts would have the power to rule on what constitutes the minimum with which people must be provided for the defined rights to be adequately met. But they could set only the minimum, not the maximum. Nothing would prevent Parliament or provincial legislatures from going further and meeting a higher standard than required by any court ruling. Governments would be prevented only from doing less, and public opinion could continue to press politicians for more and better social measures, just as it can today. A constitutional charter of social rights, consequently, could only give people enhanced, not diminished, protection by enforcing the meeting of human needs that we cannot in any event afford as a society to leave unmet.

Still, social justice in the Canada of the future will require more than just addressing the most basic needs for food, shelter, clothing and the like. We are only beginning to recognize the importance to individuals and to the proper functioning of our society of a range of broader human and community needs.

In a society where a growing percentage of the population will be elderly, people will need a variety of support services to allow them to lead full, independent and dignified lives in their old age. The specific services needed naturally vary with the individual, but will include such things as transportation, assistance with shopping, housekeeping, food preparation, recreation and leisure activities, maintenance and repairs to homes, and home-care health services.

At the other end of the age spectrum, we still have huge gaps in the availability and quality of child care. In order for all Canadians to have equality of opportunity to work outside the home, access to affordable child care has to be a social right. At the same time, we now know that the quality of care children receive in their early years has enormous impact on their long-term intellectual and emotional development, and hence on the kind of participants in society they will become as adults. We therefore have an opportunity to combine the need for child care with the benefits of early childhood education by providing children with sufficiently individualized attention in a stimulative play-learning environment.

There are pressing needs as well for expansion of other human infrastructure services in areas such as health care, integration of the disabled into society and counselling and support for people in various kinds of crisis. And if we agree that a clean and safe environment is also a fundamental social right of Canadians, it will take a great commitment of hands-on labour and effort to clean up and protect that environment.

None of our broad social needs is more important than that of ensuring employment or other meaningful involvement in the economy for every Canadian who wants it. Being relegated lastingly to the sidelines deprives people not only of an earned income but also of their sense of participation in society and ultimately their dignity. The traditional approaches to job creation no longer suffice, however, because today there is a much wider dimension to the rapid changes that are challenging our society. We have to look at such new realities as the changing nature of work, the evolving methods of distributing wealth and the shifting relationship between our society's need for full employment and its need for social services.

Throughout history, the role of human labour has been to produce the goods and services needed by a society. The more people worked, the more a society was able to consume and to export, and the higher its standard of living. Hence, anyone who did not work was regarded as not pulling his or her share. In recent decades, however, because of a combination of automation, market saturation and competition from other exporting countries, less and less of the total potential work force is required to produce all the commercial goods and services we can consume or reasonably expect to sell abroad. Work is being transformed, at least partially, from a necessity for production to a means of distributing wealth and a framework for social participation.

Employment nevertheless remains vital in our society for at least three reasons. It is the means through which individuals obtain a share in the wealth of our society and hence the money to sustain themselves, by earning an income. It gives individuals a sense of self-worth and a meaningful role in a society that defines people in terms of what they do for a living. And it gives people the money to function as consumers of goods and services, thereby creating economic activity and employment for others. Carefully analysed in this light, the call for full employment in today's economy is not so much a demand to produce more goods and services as simply to produce more jobs.

The traditional response to public pressure for more jobs has been to stimulate employment artificially in one way or another. Governments have used grants, tax breaks and other forms of subsidies to coax companies to open new factories — not so much for the sake of the production of goods as for the production of jobs. Similarly, non-viable enterprises have been kept alive with financial life-support systems to prolong employment as long as possible. In a broader sense, meanwhile, our society has supported artificially creating consumer demand and hence jobs. We have tacitly accepted built-in obsolescence in products. We have, for instance, been willing to trade in our cars every few years instead of insisting that manufacturers build vehicles that will last a quarter of a century because we have accepted that the economy cannot work that way without wiping out a lot of jobs. We also go along with advertising-induced demand for new products of at best marginal utility, for similar reasons.

All this is tremendously wasteful of money, raw materials and, perhaps most important, human resources. And it is ultimately doomed to failure as a long-term strategy. The most it can do is delay, not alter, the inevitable reality that a diminishing proportion of our total available work force will be needed in profit-oriented manufacturing and services. Our only choice is, do we close our eyes to this reality and have change happen to us by force of circumstance, or do we recognize what is happening early enough to shape the changes to the best advantage of our whole society?

Canada has a growing surplus of unemployed workers in profit-oriented manufacturing and services. Canadians have a need to feel socially useful and to earn a living. And Canada has huge and growing unmet needs in the labour-intensive "people-helping" and environmental protection fields. This convergence virtually invites us to find ways of channelling our surplus human resources toward addressing our unmet needs.

This will require not only a transfer of resources but also a major attitudinal shift. Instead of spending vast sums to attract or prop up marginally viable industries that provide a Band-Aid solution to unemployment, our long-term interests would be better served by redirecting people toward the tasks of social development that would improve the quality of life of all Canadians.

Much of the surplus labour pool is male, while many of these tasks in the people-helping fields have traditionally been regarded as "women's work" — and as such have been treated as non-prestigious, ill-paid labour. An attitudinal shift would meet human needs while breaking down gender prejudices about career choice. Women have indeed been the pioneers in establishing much of the framework of the people-caring organizations in place today. The absurd price they have paid is to have this type of work perceived as menial, while the traditionally male occupations in manufacturing and services have been much more highly prized. We need now to recognize at last that shaping a child's development in day care is certainly no less socially important than shaping a mould in a factory; that driving the elderly to the grocery store is no less prestigious than driving rivets; that assisting the disabled should be no less well paid than assisting customers in a store.

The image of retraining hard-hats into babysitters may still seem ludicrous to many. But today's reality is that we are breaking down the restrictive gender roles that in the past narrowed people's career options. Already it is no longer uncommon for men to choose the role of stay-at-home care-giver, more and more young males are choosing to work in day-care centres and paternity leave has recently been introduced for men who choose to be at home with their newborns. This trend toward breaking down the barriers to choice is increasingly being acknowledged as a natural progression toward a more enlightened and sensible development of our society.

Rather than trying to artificially create jobs as a stop-gap measure or restricting people who would prefer to work to unemployment insurance or welfare, we have the opportunity to involve people in meaningful work that will improve the quality of life of all Canadians. We have the opportunity to recognize that for the Canada of tomorrow, health care, education and social services of every kind are not rivals to the creation of wealth. On the contrary, they are necessary conditions for the creation of wealth in a new economy where a healthy, well educated and fulfilled population is the most valuable resource; and they are the payoff for successful wealth creation.

This investment in our future can be funded in part with some of the proceeds derived from a new emphasis on exporting our public and private sector knowledge and expertise in such fields as running health-care systems; planning the use of natural resources, mining and forestry; developing transportation and telecommunications networks; and establishing waste management and environmental protection systems.

Another part of the funding can come from focusing on the ways in which traditional methods for distributing income have been affected by technological change, and adapting income distribution mechanisms to ensure that society derives a fair share of wealth for public purposes. In the way our economy previously functioned, part of the income from a firm's production of goods or services was distributed to its workers through their salaries. Part of that, in turn, was distributed to society for public spending through income tax, and another part was distributed through workers' consumer spending. Another share of the income from production was obtained for society directly from the firm through corporation taxes.

To see how that distribution is changing, we need only visualize a hypothetical totally automated production plant. With no production workers, none of the income from the goods the plant produces is distributed through salaries. Consequently, no share of the income is obtained by society through workers' income tax or consumer spending. If we assume that the plant is foreign-controlled — as are the majority of manufacturing plants in Canada — there is also no prospect of obtaining a reasonable portion of the income for society through income tax on shareholders who receive the firm's dividends. Most of those dividends will be paid, and taxed, in another country.

The only other basis for distributing a share of income from this hypothetical firm's production is through corporate taxes. But in fact we have been moving away from this form of taxation. Corporate income taxes, as a portion of total federal tax revenues, have plunged from 26 per cent in the mid-1970s to as low as 8 per cent in recent years.

The example of a totally automated plant is obviously the extreme case, although some such facilities already exist. But the phenomenon it illustrates is real to whatever degree automation makes it possible to produce the same or greater value of output with fewer workers. We cannot distribute to society a share of that increased profit by taxing the non-existent incomes of the workers who were displaced to make it possible, nor can we obtain sales tax from consumption that those displaced workers can no longer afford.

What we can do, and need to do, is change the emphasis in our tax system to enable it to gain for society a fair share of the employment-less wealth generated by automation in the commercial manufacturing and service sectors. After all, those enterprises are of no value to us unless our society can obtain a fair share of the wealth they produce. That share, in turn, could be used to help expand the needed provision of employment and services in the human-care fields.

None of this, of course, constitutes a detailed blueprint for making the transition to a society that fully takes advantage of changing labour market conditions to meet human needs and promote social justice while providing hope for the future. The essential first step is simply to recognize the changes that are taking place and the direction in which we should be moving. Once we do that, we can mobilize all our considerable resources — in the public service, in universities, in think-tanks and in the private sector — to devise the necessary strategies and mechanics for achieving our goal.

If we are bold in our faith in our values and resolute in our national will to adapt to change, we Canadians have the potential to become an example to the world of how prosperity, social justice and a high quality of life for every citizen can work hand in hand, all reinforcing each other.

TWELVE

Prosperity Within Our Means

"**B**UT WHAT ABOUT THE DEFICIT?" That question has come to be used as a way to abruptly end, rather than begin, any discussion of creative new initiatives for Canada's future. If, as the Tories and many in the business community insist, the deficit is already such an overwhelming problem that we have no choice but to keep cutting back, how can we possibly afford to move ahead with any of the new things that need to be done?

The question really needs to be turned around: How can we afford *not* to invest in our immediate economic survival and future prosperity?

We know what the choices are. Either we compete internationally through the excellence of our knowledge and skills, or we slip into Third World conditions through the cheapness of our labour and the meanness of our working environment. To avoid the latter, we must invest now in education, training and research and development, as all our key competitors are beginning to do.

We know, as all our competitors know, that competitiveness in this new world economy requires that brainpower be supplemented by an excellent national infrastructure of transportation and communications. The quality of our links to one another and to the world — our roads, railways, airports, computer networks, fibre-optic cables and other telecommunications links — will be a crucial determinant of our success. Canada has been severely neglecting the maintenance and improvement of this infrastructure, and even cutting back parts of it, while our competitors are investing in improving theirs.

And we know that in an economy where people are the most valuable asset, excellent health care and strongly supportive social programs are critically important investments in human capital. Today we have a million and a half Canadians unemployed, we have more than a million children living in poverty and we are in the midst of the worst economic collapse since the Great Depression. Unless we act urgently to address these immediate problems, many workers who are jobless today will never work again and young people now leaving school may spend a decade in deepening hopelessness before ever getting their first meaningful job. The social and economic damage will be beyond repair.

Knowing all this, how can we possibly justify digging ourselves ever deeper into a hole by fixating exclusively on the deficit, as the Tories have been doing since they came to power? The federal deficit is undoubtedly a legitimate concern. But to see it as the *sole* concern is to distort economic planning, needlessly subject ourselves to devastating hardship and sabotage our children's future. When we weigh the costs of necessary deficit spending against the costs of inaction, the answer seems clear.

Any competent business person knows that there is nothing wrong with incurring debt, as long as the borrowing is used for investment that will generate more wealth over time. That sort of prudent borrowing for investment is very different from borrowing for immediate consumption on day-to-day expenditures. It is the difference between borrowing to buy technologically advanced equipment or borrowing repeatedly just to meet the payroll. Government accounting methods don't distinguish between expenditures on day-to-day operations and expenditures that are investments in upgrading Canada's human capital or physical infrastructure. But the additional deficit spending that is required now — spending on education, training, research and development, health care, social programs and upgrading our infrastructure while creating immediate jobs — all falls into the investment category.

Much of today's rhetoric overlooks the fact that government deficits are, in themselves, neither good nor bad. Nor is there any absolute, fixed size of deficit that is appropriate. Deficits are merely instruments of economic policy that must be assessed at any given time in the context of the overall state of the economy, the society's needs and the alternatives to running a deficit of any given size.

But Conservatives and many leaders of big business approach the whole issue of the deficit from a strangely distorted perspective. They have succeeded in selling a great many Canadians on the premise that, in principle, deficits are bad and balanced budgets are good. A government that spends more in any year than it takes in, they argue, is by definition living beyond its means and irresponsibly mortgaging our future. Presented with this argument in terms of the metaphor of a household that fails to live within its budget, Canadians understandably relate to it.

But the reality, of course, is that governments are not households. And households, in any event, do borrow money for reasonable and valid purposes. So do businesses. A family that takes out a mortgage to buy a home or gets a bank loan to buy a car is not living beyond its means, provided it can reasonably expect to have the income to meet the payments. As for business, by far the biggest critic of government deficits, few if any corporations operate without borrowing huge sums of money themselves. Expansions and takeovers are financed not from current operating revenues, but by incurring debt.

When companies make investments with borrowed money, or families buy homes with mortgages, we are told that this is sound financial planning. Yet the idea of comparable government borrowing for investment in people or in infrastructure is depicted by the Tories and big business as wild-eyed irresponsibility. On the contrary, such deficit spending by the national government is not only justified in our current circumstances, it is absolutely vital.

To argue otherwise is to insist on trapping ourselves in a vicious circle. By the Tories' own logic, we have the existing deficit largely because Canada is so uncompetitive that we don't have enough economic prosperity to provide sufficient tax revenues to sustain government spending. But because of that same deficit, the Tories and their supporters insist, we cannot afford to spend on precisely those investments that would make us more competitive. That approach is, quite simply, a prescription for despair and endless deterioration. If obsession with the deficit continues to block needed investment, five or ten years from now the result will be an undereducated, unhealthy, socially troubled country with a crumbling infrastructure. Such a society has nowhere to go but down in a globally competitive world, and its decline can only lead either to higher deficits in the future or to further crippling spending cuts that continue the downward spiral.

The prospect of such a decline reveals the fundamental flaw in the argument that deficits irresponsibly saddle our children with a debt that imperils their future. The reality is quite the opposite. If we invest intelligently now in ensuring that our children will come of age equipped with knowledge, skills, health and confidence in a Canada that has a high degree of social stability and all the physical facilities needed for sustained economic development, we will be endowing them with a promising future. They can have a prosperity that will make today's deficits seem irrelevant. It is by doing less that we would be robbing them of their birthright.

The argument that Canada simply cannot afford the necessary expenditures because of the size of the national debt has not been persuasively made. The Tories make much of the fact that the federal government currently spends 36.5 cents out of every tax dollar it receives on financing its debt — much more than our major competitor nations. But such comparisons are misleading, because they look at the tax receipts and expenditures of only national governments. Canada is a federal state, which means that not only the central government but also the provinces collect taxes and are capable of having debts or surpluses. When one looks at the total picture for all levels of government in Canada, it turns out that interest payments on debt work out to 22 cents out of every tax dollar — a figure roughly similar to Japan's 20 cents. And no one suggests that Japan is in danger of going broke.

The reality, as well, is that most of the deficit and most of the federal government's debt payments are a matter of borrowing from *ourselves*. To the degree that the government's deficit is financed through bonds and other loan instruments held by Canadian individuals and institutions, rather than by foreign lenders, money is simply being recycled through our own economy. It's not as if all those interest payments were being siphoned out of the country. The Mulroney government has been increasing the proportion of borrowing done abroad, but the fact remains that right now more than 60 per cent of Canadian government bonds are held within Canada. So while the government is paying 36.5 cents of every tax dollar in interest payments, 22 of those cents are being paid to Canadians. Borrowing from ourselves, through our own government, to finance vitally needed national expenditures is hardly the recklessness that critics of deficit spending make it seem.

In any event, the Mulroney government's strategy for dealing with the deficit simply doesn't work. Since a deficit is the excess of expenditures over revenues, when revenues are high the deficit can come down even while spending remains constant or increases. But the consequence of Tory policies has been a steadily deteriorating economy in which fewer people are employed and there is less economic activity for the government to tax. The inescapable result is lower revenues for government. Until recently, economic slowdowns also meant higher costs for the federal government because of increased payouts for unemployment insurance and welfare. The Mulroney government, however, has transferred this burden to others — to provincial governments by limiting the federal share of welfare payments, and to workers and employers by withdrawing from paying its part of the cost of UIC. But this is little more than an accounting trick. Containing the federal deficit by shifting the burden to the provinces and forcing *them* to run higher deficits — or by making workers and employers pay what would have been the government's bill for the recession — does nothing to improve the overall picture.

The more the federal government tries to counteract the recession's effect on its revenues by cutting spending or raising the taxes paid by ordinary Canadians — most recently through imposing the GST — the worse it makes the situation. Taking more money out of circulation in the economy reduces the demand for goods and services, slowing economic activity further, throwing still more people out of work, further reducing the government's tax income and increasing the social costs that must be borne by one level of government or another. As a prescription for reducing the deficit or restoring economic health, this approach is the financial equivalent of the long-discredited medical "remedy" of bleeding an already-anemic patient.

None of this means that the deficit can be allowed to rise limitlessly or in perpetuity. But the way to bring it down in an orderly fashion, over time, is through a balanced approach to economic management. We have to recognize, first of all, that nothing brings down a deficit like prosperity, coupled with a fair approach to taxation. Unless we do what is necessary to restore prosperity, deficits will keep increasing — and they will be the least of our problems. And unless the tax system is reviewed to ensure that, as the economy improves, those who can afford it most — the wealthiest individuals and the most profitable corporations — will pay their fair share, our opportunity to bring down the deficit will be squandered.

Contrary to what many people believe, Canada as a whole has not been an over-taxed nation by international standards. Excluding the impact of the recently introduced GST, government tax revenues as a percentage of gross domestic product have consistently been lower in Canada than in Germany, Britain, France and a majority of the other 22 leading industrialized nations in the Organization for Economic Co-operation and Development (OECD). And, in terms of the level and quality of services provided by governments, Canadians have been receiving — at least until recently — far better value for their money than people in most other countries.

Our problem is not excessive taxation, but inequitable and ineffective taxation. More and more of the tax burden has been shifting from corporations to individuals, and from the most affluent individuals to middle-income Canadians. Taxes on individuals account for a much higher proportion of total tax revenues in Canada than they do in any of our major trading partners. The argument that corporations would flee Canada if they were required to bear a fairer share of the total tax burden, becomes much less persuasive when we consider that in a country like Japan the share of total government tax revenues paid by corporations is almost three times as large as in Canada.

Ordinary Canadians have historically not objected too much to taxation, as long as they perceived that the system was basically fair and that they were getting good programs and services in return. Today, however, the perception of fairness has evaporated as a result of Tory policies, and so has the sense of getting value for money.

Ordinary people find themselves paying more and more taxes, getting less and less in return as a result of the federal government's incessant cutbacks, and still seeing the deficit — the supposed reason for all this hardship — remain high. People understandably feel that they are being cheated, and that their money is going down the drain. If we allow such feelings to persist and grow, we risk creating not only a tax revolt but a worsening breakdown in social consensus and faith in government.

A balanced approach to rebuilding prosperity while bringing the deficit under control must also focus on interest-rate policy. Were it not for its interest payments on the debt, the federal government would currently have a budget surplus, not a deficit — and those interest payments have in recent years been much higher than they need to be. Canadian interest rates have historically tended to be no more than a few points higher than rates in the U.S. The Mulroney government, however, has had a policy of favouring astronomically high interest rates to fight inflation and to keep our dollar at an artificially elevated level. In 1990, for instance, Canadian real short-term interest rates of 10.9 per cent were more than double the rates in the U.S., Germany and Japan. This insistence on unnecessarily high interest rates has had the effect of adding billions of dollars a year to the interest payments the government must make — and therefore to the size of the deficit and the national debt.

A sustained policy of restoring the historic spread between Canadian and U.S. interest rates would bring down the deficit both directly and indirectly. Directly, it would reduce the federal government's own debt-servicing payments. Indirectly, it would stimulate economic activity — and hence tax revenues — by reducing the cost of borrowing for businesses and consumers. Business activities, employment and government tax income would also increase as the Canadian dollar came down from the artificially high levels at which it has been propped by excessive interest rates, making the price of our exports of goods and services more competitive abroad.

By relying on this more creative mix of economic management policies to bring the deficit under control, we would free ourselves to undertake the investments that our immediate and long-term prosperity requires. Beginning immediately to invest in upgrading and expanding our infrastructure, coupled with lowered interest rates and a more realistically valued dollar, would put many Canadians back to work, restore vitality to our economy and set us firmly on a course toward enhanced competitiveness.

THIRTEEN

Freeing Ourselves From Free Trade

T O FULFIL OUR DESTINY AS A NATION, we must first be free. We cannot move forward as a knowledge-intensive, healthy, prosperous, innovative and socially progressive people while shackled by a Canada–U.S. trade agreement that ties our hands in virtually every respect.

The essential first step to building our future is inescapably clear: we must reclaim our freedom to choose our own directions and resuscitate our ability to survive economically. We must abrogate the free trade deal.

Until we invoke our agreed-upon right to terminate the deal, we will not be able to break away from the Tory version of "competitiveness" that dooms us to ever-declining wages and work conditions, vanishing jobs and a self-destructing economy. We will be unable to pursue the alternative vision of competitiveness that begins with developing an effective national industrial strategy. We will be unable to throw all our energies into becoming the knowledge-intensive economy and the socially progressive society that should be the birthright of our children. We will be unable to use government on our behalf, as we have successfully done throughout our history, to shape our economic and social renewal. We will, in short, be unable to become more and more Canadian in our approach to the challenges of the future, instead of less and less.

Because the free trade agreement forces us to harmonize our economic and social policies with those of the United States. Because it deprives us of the option of establishing new Crown corporations or using other forms of major government intervention to meet national goals. Because it robs us of exclusive control over our own energy and natural resources. Because it prevents us from ensuring Canadian ownership of key sectors of our economy, such as financial institutions. Because it removes our right to impose performance requirements that are in our national interest on U.S. multinational corporations operating in Canada. Because it is already bleeding our economy dry with plant closures and job losses. Because none of the benefits that we were promised would flow from the deal are occurring and because all the harmful consequences we were told couldn't happen are happening. Because it is destroying our self-confidence and our very will to be Canadian. For all these reasons — and for many, many more — sheer common sense must tell us to free ourselves from this deal before the damage beomes irreparable.

Some critics of the deal argue that we should at least try first to renegotiate its provisions, saving abrogation as a last resort if this attempt fails. That approach certainly appeals to the traditional Canadian instinct for compromise and for incremental rather than abrupt action. But no good, and much harm, would be sure to result from timid half-measures in this instance.

Nothing in the American bargaining style in the original negotiations gives the slightest reason to believe the United States would be prepared to make major concessions now out of altruistic concern for the problems we are experiencing. Any renegotiation would inevitably entail hard-nosed bargaining by the Americans that required us to give something new away for every alteration they accepted, if indeed they accepted any. But Mulroney has already given away all our bargaining chips. Trading one damaging provision for some new, equally or more damaging one would scarcely put us ahead of the game.

In any event, the deal is so fundamentally flawed that the modification of a few of its worst provisions could not transform it into being in Canada's best interests. In a renegotiated deal, would the Americans agree to restore to us exclusive control over the use and pricing of our energy and natural resources? Would they agree to a Canadian definition of subsidy that explicitly exempts our social programs, our regional development programs and our measures to protect Canadian culture? Would they agree to our sovereign right to block all foreign takeovers we consider contrary to our best interests? Would they agree to our right to help our own Canadian companies more than foreign-owned ones to become internationally competitive through government contracts and the like? Would they agree to give Canadian goods and services genuinely assured access to the United States market by exempting us from the application of U.S. trade laws? Anyone who believes that the Americans might make any, let alone all, of these concessions probably also believes that Elvis is still alive.

It is equally illusory to believe that unsuccessfully renegotiating first, and then abrogating only afterward, would somehow be perceived as more courteous by the United States. If we did try to renegotiate, one of two unfortunate outcomes would result.

The United States might make so few concessions, or such minor ones, that Canada would have no choice but to walk away from the table and abrogate the deal. That would be likely to antagonize the Americans even more than a straight-up abrogation from the outset. By then, they would have invested considerable time and attention in the process and would have threatened Canada with retaliation if we rejected their token offers. They would then feel compelled to make good on those threats if we indeed cancelled the deal. Alternatively, our government might feel compelled to avert such a retaliatory outcome by accepting whatever the Americans offered and proclaiming a great victory. After an initial period of relief that free trade had been improved, Canadians would discover that the most damaging elements remained intact and we were in fact no better off. And even if some subsequent Canadian government were to contemplate abrogation, by then the integration of our economies and the erosion of our independent identity would have proceeded so far that there would scarcely be any point.

Our best option is to invoke the six-month provision to cut off the deal with surgical precision while we still have our vital resources intact. Mulroney himself insisted emphatically during the leaders' debate in the 1988 election that the deal was "a simple commercial transaction cancellable on six months' notice." We can rightly point out to the Americans that abrogation is in the contract precisely to enable either party to withdraw if the deal no longer appears beneficial. Since it clearly is not beneficial to us, it is as appropriate for us to invoke this provision as it would be for the Americans if they felt disadvantaged. There would be no reason for them to retaliate, though that would not necessarily dissuade them from doing so.

Political realities being what they are, there's no denying that we would likely pay a short-term price for abrogation. But that risk should not be blown out of proportion. Some people argue that there would be a massive flight of capital from Canada if we terminated the deal. It is hard to see the logic of that suggestion. There might well be some short-term disruption, simply because capital tends to respond nervously to *any* change. But there was no shortage of underlying confidence in Canada before free trade came into being. Capital was not massively fleeing Canada because we lacked a free trade deal. Nor, when Mulroney initially came to power as a prime minister supposedly opposed to free trade, was there any such flight. So there is no reason to believe there would be a major and lasting collapse of confidence after the demise of a deal that is so clearly detrimental to the Canadian economy. We also should not allow the prospect of ending the deal to be misrepresented as protectionism. There is nothing "protectionist" about relying on the world's multilateral trading system rather than becoming part of "Fortress America."

As for fears that the United States would set out to punish us economically for ending the deal, the American capacity for retaliation is limited by the international General Agreement on Tariffs and Trade (GATT), which prohibits discriminatory trade practices. As well, since Canada is the United States' largest single export market, it is not in the best interest of the Americans to throw their own people in exporting industries out of work by bringing our economy to its knees.

The kinds of things the U.S. is most likely to do to us in retaliation if we abrogate the trade deal, it is already doing anyway. As Gordon Ritchie, the Canadian deputy chief negotiator of the agreement, has pointed out: "There is mounting evidence that the U.S. administration and Congress are simply unprepared to honour the spirit or, in some cases, even the letter itself of the free trade agreement." Areas in which the United States has been hampering our exports in violation of the agreement already include softwood lumber, plywood, red meat and pork, and cars. The Americans' behaviour is both a demonstration of the futility of the deal and an indication that they couldn't treat us much worse in its absence. In any event, fears of U.S. retaliation if we assert our basic prerogatives as an independent nation need to be kept in perspective. In other parts of the world, people have been willing to lie down in front of tanks to demand their rights to have a free and independent country. What would it say of us as Canadians if we are paralysed by fear that if we reclaim our sovereignty the Americans might hit us with a tariff on hog bellies?

Conversely, abrogating the deal would be a crucial psychological breakthrough at this point in our history. Quite apart from the economic and political imperatives that require abrogation, acting decisively to free ourselves from free trade would break the paralysis of national will that has been afflicting us. It would restore to Canadians the sense of having the means to control our own destiny and the faith that we can build a future even better than our past. Ending the deal is the indispensable first step to a new beginning for our nation.

FOURTEEN

Healing Our Future

T O BE ABLE TO MOVE INTO THE FUTURE with
a clear conscience and renewed pride in
Canada, we must urgently remedy the most
glaring injustice of our past. Our treatment of Canada's
indigenous peoples throughout our history is a national
shame, an affront to our vision of ourselves as a decent
and moral nation.

Long before the first European settlers crossed the
Atlantic, the original citizens of Canada had a rich and
vibrant culture, a profound spirituality and deeply held
social values based on respect for the earth and all forms
of life. The political structures that existed in the aboriginal nations were so highly developed that the
Iroquois Confederacy served as the model for the first
democratic systems of government in Europe, and for
concepts of federalism, on both of which our own system today is based. It was the indigenous population's
support and sharing of knowledge that enabled the earliest European settlers to survive in Canada's harsh
environment. We had, and continue to have, much to
learn from the first nations people. Their full participation in our national life, and our willingness to respect
their culture, can be mutually enriching and beneficial.

Instead our society, through our government, has taken away the lands of aboriginal people, broken solemn commitments that were made to them, tried deliberately to eradicate their culture and reduced them to living today in Third World conditions. We have come perilously close to destroying an entire people. It is a testament to the strength of the aboriginal nations and their culture that they have *not* been broken or assimilated despite all they have endured. But they have paid, and are still paying today, a terrible price for their determination to hold on to their identity.

The infant mortality rate on reserves is twice as high as in the rest of Canada. Aboriginal children who survive infancy are four times as likely to die by the age of 14 as are non-native children. Third World diseases such as tuberculosis and gastroenteritis — diseases that have been all but eradicated in the rest of Canada — are still a major cause of death on reserves. More than 36 per cent of housing on reserves is overcrowded, compared with only 2 per cent elsewhere. Half the dwellings on reserves have no central heating, and a third have no running water. The average income on reserves is one-third that of other Canadians. The conditions in which native peoples live are so appalling that even Archbishop Desmond Tutu, who has spent a lifetime witnessing the squalor of black townships in South Africa, was shocked. Visiting an Ojibway reserve in Ontario in 1990, he observed that the people are forced to live "as if they were dirt. It distresses me. How is it possible anywhere?"

It is scarcely surprising that tragically large numbers of aboriginal people, particularly the young, choose *not* to live like this. The suicide rate among natives under the age of 25 is six times higher than among non-native youth. Fully one-third of all deaths among native teenagers are suicides. Researchers believe that the overall suicide rate among natives is as much as 12 times the national average, which makes it one of the highest in the world. Great numbers of aboriginal Canadians are choosing to die rather than to live in the conditions our policies have imposed on them. How can we live with ourselves if we allow this to continue?

The suicide rate among natives is the ultimate symptom of a society that for generations has been subjected to almost unbearable stress Many of those who don't kill themselves outright try to deaden themselves with alcohol or substance abuse. These are the consequences of dependency and despair. The whole thrust of Canadian policy until recently has been to strip first nations people of control over their own lives. To this day, to live on a reserve is to be virtually powerless.

Aboriginal people are denied ultimate authority over almost everything that touches their lives, since every decision or bylaw passed by a locally elected band council is subject to approval or veto by the federal Department of Indian and Northern Affairs. The federal government can limit hunting and fishing on reserves. Under the Indian Act, the federal government can transfer land from a reserve to a provincial government or a corporation without the consent of the natives who live on that land. That's because the act specifies that even the land on their own reserves does not legally belong to the aboriginal people but rather to the federal government. Until as recently as 1960, native Canadians were not even allowed to vote in federal elections; the last province to allow natives to vote in provincial elections — Quebec — only did so in 1969.

Not only have natives been kept powerless over their own lives, until very recently their culture was under deliberate and direct assault by the national government. From the 19th century until the 1950s, native children were forcibly removed from their homes and sent to residential schools whose explicit purpose was to break them away from aboriginal cultures and assimilate them into white society. In these schools, they were brutally punished for speaking their own language, playing traditional native games or singing their own songs. As part of the same strategy of assimilation, even on reserves many traditional native dances and ceremonies were until the 1950s outlawed under the Indian Act, and people who took part in them were actually arrested and charged. Even when these official practices of forced assimilation were dropped, attitudes of unofficial assimilation evolved to take their place. By the early 1980s in Western Canada, for instance, nearly half of all children who were removed from their parents and put into white foster homes were aboriginal.

The consequence of official and unofficial attempts at assimilation was that the underpinnings of aboriginal society — religion, language, culture and social values based on thousands of years of tradition — were largely knocked away. Whole generations were left dispirited, alienated, robbed of their dignity and dependent on federal hand-outs.

We cannot undo all the harm that was done in the past. But we cannot be the nation we want to be unless we do everything in our power to ensure justice for aboriginal Canadians in the present and the future.

Earlier generations of Canadians succumbed to the colonial mentality of the conqueror, the arrogant belief that people who are different are by definition inferior. They saw assimilation not as something they were doing *to* the aboriginal peoples but rather *for* them. Today, we no longer have even that excuse of cultural ignorance. We now know that the Canadians who formulated these devastating policies were, in fact, dealing with a culture in many ways more highly evolved than their own. The aboriginal people, with a renewed sense of pride and confidence in their heritage and traditions, have reached the limits of their patience. The time for positive action is now.

To persist instead in our current treatment of the aboriginal people would be to cross a point of no return. It would risk eventually creating the kind of corrosive anger and generational hatred seen in too-long-oppressed people like the Palestinians, a consuming fury that makes constructive solutions increasingly impossible. There is not the slightest reason to allow that to happen. We have evolved as a country to the point where we can be united in the effort to ensure that *all* Canadians can feel equal, free, valued and respected.

It is not surprising that after such a long history of repression and marginalization, there are some native radicals who have emerged to alarm Canadians with a rhetoric of inward-turning isolation. But this approach runs counter to the mainstream thinking, tradition and values of aboriginal peoples, whose whole culture emphasizes a spirit of openness. What is most important to ordinary people in native communities, as it is to other Canadians, is the freedom and the means to control their own lives, to make their own choices and to participate in Canadian society as much or as little as they themselves choose. That freedom must reasonably include having control over their own institutions in such vital areas as education, health care, social services and the administration of justice.

An essential first step must be to entrench in the Constitution, without further delay, the right to aboriginal self-government within the framework of Canada. It makes nosense to argue that the aboriginal people must first define the details of that right before we can recognize it. It exists. It was never extinguished.

The aboriginal people have an undeniable moral and political right to exercise the jurisdictions necessary to maintain their languages, culture and traditions. Whether the exercise of that jurisdiction requires a status analogous to that of provincial government, or some more innovative approach, will have to be worked out in negotiations. But there is no reason such details cannot be elaborated *after* constitutional recognition of what is obviously just, so that people who have already waited too long will have a meaningful assurance that their right to emerge from domination will not be sloughed off for further decades or centuries.

In restoring rights, we must be careful not to take away rights at the same time. Native women, who comprise 52 per cent of the total aboriginal population, have emphatically insisted that they do not want to lose the protection of the Charter of Rights and Freedoms as a result of native self-government. Nor do they want aboriginal governments to be given the power to invoke the "notwithstanding" clause of the Charter, currently restricted to the federal and provincial governments, to override protected rights.

The aboriginal women's most direct concern is the importance of the Charter to their fight for sexual equal-

ity. Until as recently as 1985, under the Indian Act aboriginal women who married non-Indians were banished
from their communities; they and their children were
effectively cut off from their families and stripped of
their Indian status. But the same fate did not befall aboriginal men who married non-Indian women; instead
these women and the children of such marriages gained
Indian status. Aboriginal women's long political struggle
for repeal of sexually discriminatory provisions of the
Indian Act succeeded only when they were able to
threaten to use the Charter of Rights to challenge the
legislation. Although this one instance of discrimination
has been resolved, native women insist that the Charter
is essential to their ongoing struggle for sexual equality.

But they also warn that, particularly in a difficult transition period as self-government comes into effect, the
full protection of the Charter is vital for other reasons as
well. They point to other potential dangers to individual
rights in permitting any government, including newly
developing aboriginal governments, the option of suspending such freedoms as freedom of religion, freedom
of peaceful assembly, freedom of expression, freedom
from unreasonable search and seizure or freedom from
arbitrary detention.

A constitutional guarantee of the right to self-government
within the framework of Canada is an essential first step
in moving toward justice for the aboriginal people, but
in itself it is not a sufficient one. Self-government without the necessary resources to exercise it effectively
would be worse than meaningless. There must be a will
to settle aboriginal land claims fairly and quickly. And
there must be a recognition that it does not suffice to
recognize aboriginal self-government, to transfer some

lands or cash to aboriginal people in settlement of land
claims and then to wish them well. Self-government
cannot be allowed to turn into a new formula for isolat-
ing first nations people. Both because they are citizens
of this country and because we as a society are the cause
of their current plight, our national government must
accept its ongoing responsibilities. Those responsibilities will necessarily include working closely with aboriginal governments and providing the ongoing financial
transfers to enable their communities to evolve and
flourish.

As well, there should be an explicit constitutional
commitment by Canada to preserving and promoting
aboriginal languages and culture. The languages and
culture of first nations peoples have survived generations of systematic assault. It does not suffice to give
assurances that now this assault will be withdrawn. The
aboriginal people are morally entitled to restore their
linguistic and cultural heritage to the levels that existed
before the attempted assimilation. We, through our
national government, have a moral obligation to do
everything possible to support and protect their efforts.

While virtually all natives are united in their desire for
self-government, how it occurs and what it entails are subjects for debate among their own communities, and for
negotiation with the federal and provincial governments.

With openness of spirit, it cannot be beyond our ingenuity to come to agreement on approaches that will
strike a sensitive balance between ensuring that first
nations people have rightful control over their own lives
and that our country is not fragmented. If we are to
build the cohesive, progressive Canada of the future,
essential attributes of being part of Canada must contin-

ue to apply everywhere within our borders. Aboriginal governments, like other governments in Canada, can be subject to basic national standards in such vital areas as health care, access to social programs and education, while having full scope to provide services in such fields in accordance with the needs, beliefs and culture of their people.

Canada is by no means the only country to have taken over and subjugated aboriginal peoples. What can set us apart, however, is our ability to admit we were wrong and to start afresh. We can be an example to the world: the first country in this new era of awareness to negotiate amicably with aboriginal people a jointly acceptable new relationship based on justice, freedom, equality and mutual respect. In so doing, we can enrich both our national life and our national soul.

FIFTEEN

A Nation
for Its People

O F ALL THE OPPORTUNITIES and issues confronting Canada today, the Constitution is at once the most pressing and the least important. On one hand, we urgently need to resolve the current constitutional impasse, because a situation has been created where the country may fly apart unless we can defuse tensions. On the other hand, changing the Constitution is the least important of the issues that should be on our national agenda, because the economy is a far greater priority for ordinary Canadians and there objectively is very little wrong with our Constitution as it stands.

There is no doubt that the Constitution could be improved further over time, for instance by enshrining a charter of social rights. But the demonstration has yet to be made that anything in the current Constitution stands in the way of meeting the genuine needs of Canadians in any part of the country. Nor has anyone shown that any particular change, on its own merits, is urgently needed to make Canada more just, more prosperous, more united or easier to govern.

Were it not for the national unity crisis that has been created, it would be much more productive to focus our energies on developing a national industrial strategy, making the transition to knowledge-intensive competitiveness, pursuing excellence in education, extricating ourselves from the free trade deal, implementing aboriginal self-government and strengthening our social infrastructure.

But, of course, the unity crisis cannot simply be wished away. There is now an expectation of constitutional change in Quebec that must be addressed if Canada as we know it is to endure. The challenge is to strike the right, delicate balance that avoids both an impasse that could split up our country and ill-considered reforms that could make it ungovernable. If we do too little Quebecers may vote for separation, and if we do too much we could end up with a fragmented country whose central government is too weakened to hold us together.

Both these extremes are avoidable. The key lies in recognizing the distinctions between practical and emotional needs, and between the agendas of politicians and the concerns of ordinary Canadians.

The practical reality is that the Constitution in its present form has, on the whole, served this country well. Paradoxically, its inadequacies are its greatest strength. When its main provisions were drafted as the British North America Act in 1867, few of the needs of contemporary Canada could be foreseen. But far from handicapping our country, that forced us over the years to develop a uniquely flexible and creative approach to interpreting the Constitution. Under the same, basically unchanged Constitution we have seen pendulum swings between periods of intense centralization when the federal government wielded enormous power, and periods of decentralization when power shifted toward the provinces. The effect has been to endow us with a "living" Constitution that can be interpreted to meet changing needs without requiring the kind of amendment traumas we are currently experiencing.

What is true for Canada as a whole is equally the case for Quebec in particular. Far from being some sort of straitjacket that constrains Quebec's development, the current Constitution has provided a framework within which that province's language, culture and economy have flourished. Whatever Quebecers have wanted to do to strengthen their province's special character — including Draconian measures to curb the use of English — they have been able to accomplish under the current Constitution. French has never been stronger as the language of daily life and work, Quebec's cultural industries are thriving and Quebec-based corporations have in recent years achieved international stature. None of the Quebecers who so insistently demand constitutional change have troubled to explain how all this progress can have taken place if the current Constitution has not served them well.

But the constitutional concerns of ordinary Quebecers at this point are deeply rooted in emotion. They are grounded in an understandable and long-standing fear of assimilation. As a comparatively small French-speaking minority within a predominantly English-speaking country on an overwhelmingly English-speaking continent, Quebecers live in perpetual fear of being linguistically and culturally swamped. They feel that they must look out for themselves because no one else cares — that the rest of Canada does not understand, is indifferent to their fears and barely tolerates their assertions of distinctiveness.

These emotions are very strongly felt, and recognizing them as real and important is the key to resolving the whole debate. People in the province have been persuaded that the 1982 constitutional process and the failure of Meech Lake were humiliations that prove the indifference of the rest of Canada, and that Quebec remains vulnerable until and unless further changes are made. As a result, the emotional needs of Quebecers with regard to the Constitution are twofold: they want to see Quebec's special character as a linguistically and culturally distinct society explicitly recognized in the Constitution and their right to protect their language and culture clearly entrenched; and they want to see, through the rest of Canada's approach to the Constitution, a clear demonstration that they are understood, respected and welcomed within the national family.

Although these emotional needs of ordinary Quebecers are understandable, they are being manipulated by politicians, political scientists and journalists within the province who have their own, quite different, agenda. Quebec already has virtually all the instruments it needs to protect its language and culture. But these opinion leaders insist that it is nevertheless necessary to transfer a vast list of specific federal powers to Quebec. They present Quebec's separation from Canada as a desirable, economically profitable and relatively painless alternative if such transfers of power are not forthcoming.

That benign depiction of separation or sovereignty association is as deceptive as it is absurd. It fails to take into account the devastating emotional, economic, social and political forces that would be unleashed if our country were abruptly torn apart, against the wishes of its majority. A nation forced to negotiate its own break-up would not be kindly disposed toward those who have imposed on it this calamity. Complex negotiations over the terms of separation would almost certainly be caught up in a backlash of bitterness and hostility. The rest of Canada, having been decisively rejected by Quebec, would be in no mood to care about the former province's needs or concerns, let alone to enter into any association deals that would treat the new entity as anything close to an equal.

Whether or not Canada would be able to regroup and survive as a shadow of its former self, Quebec would surely find itself in precisely the situation that its people have always feared the most and have been able to avoid by being part of Canada. A separate Quebec would be totally isolated on an overwhelmingly English-speaking continent where no one any longer had a reason to care at all about the preservation of its language and culture.

Some of those who insist on a choice between massive power transfers or separation are separatists or ultra-nationalists who will be satisfied with nothing less than the dismantling of federalism, by degrees if they cannot achieve it in a single stroke. They want their own nation. Others are engaged in the traditional game of politicians everywhere, who want as much power as possible transferred to their particular domain. But they are playing this game in a uniquely explosive arena at a dangerous time in our history, because their demands play into the hands of the separatists.

Because separatist sentiment is widespread among francophone journalists — as it is among other members of Quebec's artistic and creative elites — the debate is presented to ordinary Quebecers through a distorting prism. Public opinion, as the American journalist Walter Lippmann pointed out, is "the pictures in our heads."

The only pictures the average Quebecer can have of the constitutional debate are based on what is published in the newspapers and said on radio and television. These media have incessantly been telling Quebecers that their need for security about the French language and culture and their need for proof of English Canada's good faith are inextricably tied to acceptance of Quebec's demands for new powers.

The consequence is that for ordinary Quebecers the transfer of powers has attained a powerful symbolic importance that has nothing to do with practical necessity. It makes little practical difference in people's everyday lives whether Quebec has exclusive jurisdiction over job training, whether the federal government is allowed to help promote tourism or whether unemployment insurance cheques come from Ottawa or Quebec City. It has become emotionally important to the average Quebecer to see the federal government transferring powers to Quebec, but it matters far less which or exactly how many specific powers are transferred.

The irony is that transferring too many powers to Quebec — or indeed to all the provinces — would have an effect precisely the opposite of promoting national unity. The more the Quebec government had control over all the policy areas that people in the province regard as important, the less relevant the federal government would become to Quebecers. Why would capable, ambitious Quebecers want to run for the federal Parliament if the real levers of power were in Quebec City? And why would ordinary Quebec citizens care much about what the federal government was doing if the issues that touch their lives were only in the hands of their provincial politicians?

In such a scenario, a kind of vicious circle would become inevitable. The less Quebec had top-quality, high-powered people representing it in the national Parliament and in the top echelons of the federal public service, the less sensitive and responsive the federal system would be to the concerns of Quebecers. And the more that Quebecers perceived the federal government to be insensitive and remote, the more they would be inclined to regard their provincial government as their only real representative. Over time, Quebec would become ever more inward looking and the rest of Canada ever more indifferent to Quebec's needs.

The foundations of our nationhood would be steadily eroded, until Quebecers eventually would have very reasonable cause to ask themselves why they bothered remaining part of an increasingly alien country when Quebec was already functioning, for all intents and purposes, as an independent nation. And if powers were similarly transferred not only to Quebec but to all the provinces, as the Tories have proposed, we would see the same phenomenon multiplied ten times over. The federal government would become irrelevant in *every* province, and Canada would in effect become a non-viable collection of mini-countries.

Just as Quebecers have an emotional need for both a sense of security about the preservation of their language and culture and a sense of acceptance by the rest of Canada, so too Canadians in other provinces have valid and important needs that have come to focus on the Constitution. People in the West and in Atlantic Canada have long felt treated like the junior partners in Confederation. They want constitutional assurance that their interests will not continue to be overshadowed by the greater economic and political clout of central Canada. But unlike the mood that has been fostered in Quebec, they want this done not so much by transferring powers from the federal government to their provincial governments as by strengthening the role of their provinces within the central government. Indeed, Canadians in every province outside Quebec share a concern that the national government not be unduly weakened and that Quebec not be given special status of a kind that would undermine the basic governmental structure of our country.

An additional emotional element that has been developing is a sense that if we must have constitutional change, we might as well go for broke. The last thing people wanted after 1982 was a new round of emphasis on the Constitution. But the nation was dragged into it and then excluded from any real say in the matter as the Meech Lake fiasco was carried out by politicians behind closed doors. Amid the resulting angry reassertion that the Constitution belongs to all Canadians, the process has gone to the other extreme and turned into a free-for-all. Everybody has a pet scheme for what should be done with the Constitution. In fact, the general frustration with government and with our growing national malaise has led to a sense among many people that we can somehow solve our problems by reinventing the country through wholesale constitutional reform. This perception has been fed by constitutional "professionals" — politicians, bureaucrats, academics, lawyers and so on — for whom the process has taken on a life of its own.

But trying to cobble together a whole new constitutional vision, particularly at this point in our history, would be a dangerous mistake. A Constitution cannot create consensus; it can only reflect consensus that already exists. At this point, we are a long way from widespread agreement on ways in which the basic structures of our country should be significantly changed, if indeed they should be significantly changed at all. The bottom line is that there is nothing fundamentally wrong with our country or our Constitution. It is just our current federal government that is fundamentally flawed, and the remedy for that lies not at the constitutional bargaining table but at the ballot box.

In a perfect world, this would be an ideal time for us to declare a five-year moratorium on all constitutional haggling. Our sense of who we are as a nation has been so profoundly shaken by the various traumas inflicted on us by the Mulroney government that we need most of all to regain our balance and our confidence, not to suffer the further strains of constitutional debates. People everywhere, including Quebec, are emotionally wrung out. They are above all stressed almost beyond endurance by the crumbling of our economy and the disintegration of employment prospects. Why put the very existence of our country, and the fate of Quebec, at risk by dealing with complex and emotionally explosive issues when everyone's nerves are already so frayed? The promise that the Constitution would not even be mentioned again for a few years, until other priorities had been addressed and we were in a healthier emotional state to achieve consensus, could well be a step toward national healing. If even a single leading politician within Quebec had the courage and vision to support this approach, Quebecers might well join with the rest of Canada in welcoming such a respite.

Since that is not about to happen, what we need at this fragile point in our history is a very focused approach to constitutional change. The more we stick to the essentials, the likelier we are to achieve clarity of purpose. Once we recognize that the key needs to be met are perceptual and emotional ones, and the key concerns to be addressed are those of ordinary people rather than of politicians, it becomes clear that the changes required, while important, are few in number.

Above all, Quebecers' fear of assimilation must be recognized and addressed. Those constitutional changes that demonstrably relate directly to the protection of the French language and culture in Quebec should be implemented in a spirit of respect and understanding. But those are the only changes to which the Quebec government, on behalf of its people, has a reasonable claim. There is no justification for other transfers of power that do not meet this criterion — transfers that would accomplish nothing but chipping away at national unity and effectiveness and that would ultimately threaten the very survival of Canada. While Canadians in other provinces must understand Quebecers' fear of assimilation, the people of Quebec in turn can reasonably be asked to understand the rest of Canada's fear of dismantling our country by degrees. Quebec is afraid of being assimilated; the rest of Canada is afraid of being devastated.

To reflect the true nature of Canada, it is entirely appropriate that our Constitution formally enshrine the prodominantly French-speaking character and cultural uniqueness of Quebec — and, even more important, that it commit our nation as a whole to ensuring that these characteristics will always endure. Not only the government of Quebec, but all of Canada, must be the guarantor that Quebecers will not be linguistically or culturally assimilated.

In doing this, the deeply felt need of Quebecers to be explicitly acknowledged within the Constitution as a "distinct society" must be met. That wording is not ideal as constitutional language because it is unnecessarily ambiguous and has taken on all kinds of emotional baggage as a result of the Meech Lake fiasco. But precisely because it has taken on emotional and symbolic significance for Quebecers, we must incorporate it in the Constitution while minimizing the potential for misunderstanding.

Taken at face value, the term "distinct society" is simply a statement of fact. Quebec is manifestly distinct in its language, in its culture, in its civil law and in the essential fact of having been a founding partner in the creation of Canada. This does not detract from the reality that *every* region of Canada is distinct from every other region. An Ontarian visiting Newfoundland would certainly have a sense of being in a distinct society, as would a Nova Scotian travelling in British Columbia. That is why we have a federal system of government under which we acknowledge regional diversity by providing all the provinces with jurisdiction over fields that are important to maintaining their local distinctiveness. But Quebecers — understandably, from their point of view — want recognition that their distinctness goes beyond being a province like the others. A long history of being dominated economically in their own province by an English-speaking business community, of feeling treated like second-class citizens and of such slights as not even being able to communicate with the national government in their own language has left its mark on Quebecers. Those abuses have been corrected, but the emotional scars remain. Recognizing the special character of

Quebec in the Constitution can strengthen, not weaken, our country — provided that politicians are not allowed to muddy the distinction between recognition of linguistic and cultural distinctness and transfer of new legislative powers.

The problem with the Meech Lake Accord's approach to the "distinct society" clause was that it did muddy this distinction, by making it an interpretive clause for the whole Constitution, including the division of powers. That would have amounted to an undefined and open-ended transfer of powers to the Quebec government and would have further eroded our unity by setting the stage for endless jurisdictional battles.

Instead, recognition of the predominantly French-speaking character and cultural uniqueness of Quebec — and therefore of Quebec as a distinct society — should be embodied in a preamble to the Constitution that states Canada's commitment to safeguarding those characteristics. This preamble, or "Canada clause" as some have called it, should celebrate who and what we are as a nation. It should recognize and articulate the founding role of aboriginal nations as the first peoples of this land. It should affirm such vital elements of our nationhood as our linguistic duality, our respect for minorities in every part of Canada, the contribution of immigrants from every part of the world, the diversity of our provinces and regions united in the pursuit of common goals, and the fundamental Canadian values to which our nation is dedicated.

It likely is also necessary to make the preservation and promotion of Quebec's character as a linguistically and culturally distinct society an interpretive clause for the Charter of Rights and Freedoms, as has been proposed. Quebecers have a much more collectivist view of the balance between individual rights and group rights than do Canadians in other parts of the country. It would be futile to try to persuade Quebecers, at this point in their history, that individual considerations take precedence over the preservation of the French language and culture if they perceive it to be threatened.

In principle, all Canadians should have the same basic rights from coast to coast. But the practical reality is that the Quebec government, like all the provincial governments, already has the power to override provisions of the Charter through the "notwithstanding" clause. Quebec has already used this power, to bypass the Supreme Court's ruling that the province's language law violates the Charter. If the "distinct society" becomes an interpretive clause in the Charter, it isn't likely to make much real-life difference in the protection accorded to individual rights in Quebec. The Quebec government will simply have another mechanism to do what it can already do with the "notwithstanding" clause.

To French-speaking Quebecers, however, the symbolic difference is important. Using the "notwithstanding" clause puts the emphasis each time on Quebec's violation of individual rights rather than on its exercise of collective rights, and Quebecers find this humiliating. Since this irritant to Quebec can be removed without significantly diminishing anyone's rights, there is little practical sense in drawing battle lines over insisting that the Charter must take precedence over the "distinct society" clause.

At the same time this does *not* mean that there should be any erosion of the rights or treatment of French-speaking minorities in other provinces. There are people who take a disturbingly tit-for-tat view of language relations and say, "Why should we treat the French in our community any better than they treat the English in Quebec?" It would be profoundly unfair to treat people in any province as hostages for the policies of some other province. It would also be self-defeating. Canada's linguistic dualism enriches us. Most Canadians take pride in our self-image as a country that has the sophistication and imagination to officially embrace two of the world's great languages. This is, in fact, an important element of our distinctness as a nation. Our Canadian values of respect for diversity have served us well. In reaffirming our commitment to those values, we can hope that in time, once their fears of assimilation are addressed, Quebecers will feel secure enough to do likewise.

Keeping in mind that the object of the exercise is to give Quebecers a reinforced sense of security within Canada, a number of other constitutional changes are also justified. It is only fair, given the understandable concerns of Quebecers, that Quebec have a veto over constitutional changes affecting the province or federal institutions. In fact, *every* region of Canada should be protected against having constitutional changes imposed on it by the rest of the country against its will. This can best be done in the context of an amending formula that creates a regional veto. All constitutional changes would have to be approved by each of the four regions — Atlantic Canada, Quebec, Ontario and Western Canada.

That approval should require a national referendum mechanism under which a majority of the voters in *each* of the four regions would have to agree to any constitutional change for it to become law. This would give effect to the fundamental reality that the Constitution belongs to all the people of Canada, not just to the politicians. Constitutional change could not be imposed on the people of Quebec against their will, nor could it be imposed on the people of any other region of the country. By the same token, individual politicians would no longer be able to block desired changes by playing constitutional games that did not represent the will of the ordinary Canadians who are the real owners of our fundamental law.

Allaying the fears of assimilation among Quebecers also justifies giving the government of Quebec special constitutional powers over the selection and integration of immigrants into the province from outside Canada. The declining birth rate among French-speaking Quebecers in recent decades has intensified those fears of assimilation. Some Quebec demographers have been warning that, over time, francophones could become a minority in their own province.

This has led Quebecers to attach particular importance to counterbalancing the falling birth rate through immigration. They seek to do this by attracting sufficient numbers of French-speaking immigrants from abroad and by ensuring that immigrants are integrated into the French-speaking majority upon arrival. This would not, of course, prevent recent immigrants to Quebec from subsequently choosing to relocate elsewhere, or immigrants to other parts of Canada from moving to Quebec. Under no circumstances could any province be given the power to restrict the free movement of people within Canada. But a special constitutional jurisdiction over immigration from abroad would be a fair-minded recognition of Quebec's exceptional linguistic situation.

It likewise makes sense to enshrine in the Constitution Quebec's long-standing right to have three of the nine judges of the Supreme Court appointed from that province, and to guarantee the Quebec government's right to have a say in the selection of those judges. This provision would give Quebecers the assurance that an important right that already exists in practice can never be taken away. In the process, we would be correcting a bizarre constitutional anomaly — the fact that our Supreme Court has never in its history been mentioned in the Constitution. The Supreme Court exists only by virtue of the federal legislation that created it. Since this legislation creating the Supreme Court is simply an act of Parliament like any other, it theoretically could be amended by Parliament alone, without the consent of any province. Enshrining the Supreme Court in the Constitution would give Quebecers, and the rest of us, the benefit of protecting our highest court from unilateral tampering by any future federal government.

The long-standing practice of appointing Supreme Court justices in consultation with the government of their home province should also be entrenched in the Constitution. As our highest court and the ultimate arbiter of constitutional questions, it is important that the Supreme Court command the confidence of the provinces as well as of the national government. For this consultation to be meaningful, the province from which a given appointment is being made should have some way to block the selection of a judge it finds particularly objectionable. This could be accomplished by providing that each province from which an appointment is being made would have a limited veto to turn down a nominee proposed by the federal government. But to prevent any province from misusing the process and turning down everyone except whomever it wanted to put on the Court, the Constitution should specify that the veto is exhausted after a province rejects three candidates for a given vacancy. The federal government would then have to make an appointment on its own authority, as it has done until now. This sort of consultation is as far as it should go. There is no justification for effectively transferring the power to select Supreme Court justices from the federal government to the provinces, as was stipulated in the Meech Lake Accord and in Mulroney's subsequent proposals. The Quebec government itself never sought such a transfer of power in its original requirements for signing a constitutional deal. It sought only a *say* in the appointment of justices.

Judges do not sit on the Court as political representatives of their home provinces or the federal government. Their role is to interpret and shape the law on behalf of *all* Canadians from coast to coast. No one has brought forward any persuasive evidence that the Supreme Court in its current form is not functioning well, nor even that any judges objectionable to their provincial governments have ever been appointed. The sole criterion for selecting the justices should be excellence, and there is no indication this criterion has not been followed in the past. A limited veto over candidates selected in consultation with the provinces should suffice to reassure provincial governments that the system will continue to function fairly in the future. The Supreme Court in its current form has served us well. If it's not broken, why fix it?

Something else that has worked well for ordinary Canadians and has no apparent need of fixing is the federal spending power. Of the Quebec government's original pre–Meech Lake conditions for accepting a constitutional deal, the only one that has no obvious connection with the protection of the French language and culture is the call for restricting the federal spending power in areas of provincial jurisdiction. This power has enabled the federal government, on our behalf, to develop vital national programs in such fields as old age pensions, medicare, social welfare and post-secondary education. It is essential if we are to develop national initiatives in such fields as day care, environmental protection, technology or a coast-to-coast upgrading of education in the future.

When a national need is identified, the federal government can use its spending power to initiate a shared-cost program with clear minimum standards of performance that serve the broad Canadian interest. As an incentive to each province to participate in the program, the government offers to contribute a substantial portion of the costs, provided the national standards are met. This is the only lever available to the federal government to ensure that Canadians across the country can enjoy the same level of vital services.

Provincial governments have long complained that this use of the federal spending power sometimes forces them into expenditures they would prefer not to make. Once the national government has introduced a program that the public finds desirable, it becomes very difficult for a province to stay out of it without incurring the wrath of its voters. This argument, however, overlooks that the reason a government is compelled by its electorate to participate in any such program is because it meets a real and important need among the people. That is why the federal government would have initiated the program in the first place. The provincial objection to shared-cost programs, consequently, is one that puts the preferences of politicians ahead of the needs of ordinary Canadians, on whose behalf government is supposed to exist.

The government of Quebec, and the governments of some other provinces, want in effect to wipe out this federal power to initiate and fund programs. They want instead a constitutional guarantee that they will receive the same federal funding whether or not they participate in a federal program. This amounts to saying, "Just give us the money, we'll decide what to do with it." They want this to be accomplished by a constitutional provision entitling any province that refuses to participate in a federal shared-cost program to receive the money anyway in "compensation," provided only that the province somehow meets the broad "objectives" of the federal program.

That would effectively mean the end of coherent nationwide programs. In the case of a program like medicare, for example, a province could take the view that the objective is simply to ensure that people are not barred from health care by lack of money. It could say that this objective can be met by only providing medicare for people earning less than $30,000, or that it can be met while permitting widespread extra-billing or deterrent fees. Or even, in a more extreme scenario, a province could distort the intent of the federal spending power by taking money intended for day care, for instance, and using it for transit systems, arguing that the objective of giving parents improved access to the workplace was being met. No national government would be likely to bother implementing a new shared-cost program if it simply meant giving provinces a pipeline into its treasury without being able to create the intended national results.

This does not mean that shared-cost programs must be absolutely identical in their implementation in every province. Allowance can be made both for regional differences and for innovative approaches tailored to the needs of a particular province. This could be achieved by constitutionally providing that a province can opt out of new shared-cost programs and receive money in compensation *if* it establishes its own program that meets specific national standards legislated by the federal Parliament.

When, prior to the Meech Lake Accord, the Quebec government set out its list of requirements for signing a constitutional deal, it cited only five: recognition of Quebec's status as a distinct society, a Quebec constitutional veto, a say in appointments to the Supreme Court, a role in immigration policy and limitation of the federal spending power. All these requirements can be met while strengthening rather than endangering Canada.

After the collapse of the Meech Lake Accord, however, the Bourassa government began producing shopping lists of areas of jurisdiction it wants transferred from the federal government to Quebec. But why would the preservation of Quebec's language and culture require transfers of power *now* that were not required a scant few years ago? No one has documented any new threats to Quebec's linguistic and cultural well-being that would call for such a shift in position. The accord fiasco, amid the overheated emotions deliberately stirred up by politicians and the Quebec media, was painful and traumatic for Quebecers. But it did not change constitutional realities, nor did it increase the powers Quebec needs to ensure the security of its language and culture.

That being the case, the failure of Meech Lake requires a new, open-spirited attempt to meet the legitimate concerns of the Quebec people. It does not require transferring powers away from the national government simply because Quebec politicians are demanding to be consoled for that failure. In fact, it would be insulting to the ordinary people of Quebec to suggest that their deeply felt emotions are to be bought off by handing out powers unrelated to language or culture as though they were constitutional trinkets. The only justification for a transfer of powers, in either direction, between the federal government and *any* province must be a clear demonstration that ordinary people will somehow be better served in practical terms by the change.

Fields of jurisdiction are not poker chips to be traded back and forth among politicians, in isolation from the concerns of ordinary Canadians. Nor is it automatically true, as many provincial politicians would have us believe, that power can best be wielded by the level of government "closest to the people." If that were the case, those same politicians would presumably be hastening to transfer powers from their own provincial governments to the municipalities. The reality, as Canada evolves and public affairs become ever more complex and interrelated, is that more and more issues are national in scope.

We cannot hope to pursue a positive vision of Canada's future unless we recognize that crucial elements of that future — elements such as education, health care, social policy, job training, communications and environmental protection — do not stop at provincial borders. To meet the needs and aspirations of an increasingly mobile Canadian population in a rapidly changing world, we require from our governments not fragmentation but coordination.

Canada has thrived under our system of government, which has been based on a careful balance of power between the federal and provincial governments. Anyone who wants to tinker with that balance should be required to demonstrate, in specific detail, why any given change would be a real improvement. That isn't what has been happening. The Quebec government has simply been putting forward demands for power transfers on the basis of some unsubstantiated entitlement. And the Mulroney government has been proposing transfers of power to the provinces, and then inviting the public and various experts to assess what these changes would do. No one has been meeting the fundamental obligation of proponents of change — the obligation to justify in clear detail why any given change is necessary, what its practical impact will be and how ordinary Canadians will be better off as a result.

The Quebec government should not be exempted from that obligation. It is up to our national government, on behalf of all Canadians, to insist that *any* premier who wants a transfer of powers must explain to the nation precisely why the existing federal exercise of those powers is harmful, and what the provincial government would want to do differently. Rather than relying on the rhetoric of self-determination as an argument, the premier of Quebec should be pressed to publicly make the case why each sought-after power would improve the well-being of the people of his province while remaining consistent with the national interest: What would Quebec do differently, for example, if it had exclusive control over job training? Over health care? Over the environment? "We want it because we want it," is not a good enough justification, for Quebec or for any other province.

As Canada continues to evolve, it may become apparent that some things currently carried out by the federal government can more effectively be done by the provinces, and vice-versa. Nothing is sacrosanct, provided the public interest remains paramount. But this period of extreme national stress, artificial deadlines and constitutional exhaustion is the worst possible time to try to make such judgments. It would be self-delusion to believe we can secure a lasting commitment to Canada among Quebecers by agreeing to measures intended to make Quebec feel as little a part of Canada as possible. What we must demand now is a national government that speaks for Canada, a government that vigorously defends the powers and responsibilities of national government instead of one that allies itself with the forces of fragmentation and dismemberment.

The determination to strengthen Canada, not weaken it, should also be the guiding principle behind our approach to Senate reform. As in the case of the constitutional issues on which Quebec has focused, a distinction has to be made between emotional needs and practical realities. People in the West and in Atlantic Canada have long felt cut off from the levers of power. They have a strong sense that the interests of central Canada always take precedence over their own regional concerns.

The "constitutional professionals" — politicians, academics and the media — have told Canadians in these regions that the answer to their grievances is Senate reform. In particular, the idea of a "Triple-E" Senate has taken on great emotional importance as a purported way to achieve fairness and balance and give the regions a stronger voice at the centre of power. This is scarcely surprising, since the words behind all three Es are powerful emotional triggers. Who, after all, could fail to be in favour of a body that is "elected, equal and effective"? The implication of these words is that anyone who opposes such a Senate wants instead arbitrary appointment, inequality and ineffectiveness.

Just as Quebecers have been led to believe that major constitutional change is required as a test of the good faith of the rest of Canada, so too the West and Atlantic Canada have come to see drastic Senate reform as a test of the good faith of Ontario and Quebec toward them. But investing too much hope in Senate reform as a cure-all for every frustration and grievance can only lead to disappointment. In fact, we risk creating more problems than we solve. There is no doubt that, with careful thought and a fully evolved consensus, the Senate can be updated and improved from its present form. But even having a Senate in which every province had equal representation would not, and should not, prevent there being occasions when the broad national interest would have to outweigh the interest of a particular province or region. And while it would not solve the problems it was intended to address, creation of a Senate strong enough to rival the House of Commons would risk paralysing the national government to the detriment of us all.

Western advocates of a Triple-E Senate cite the Trudeau government's National Energy Program (NEP) of the early 1980s as an example of a regionally detested policy that a reformed Senate would have been able to block. The simple fact, however, is that there were more energy-consuming provinces concerned about soaring oil prices in a time of supply crisis than there were energy-producing provinces concerned about getting the highest price for their resource. Even if every province had had the same number of senators and the Senate had possessed the political legitimacy to vote down the NEP, it is difficult to see why producing provinces would not have been outvoted anyway by the senators from consuming provinces.

If we turn the Senate into a chamber dedicated to regional interests rather than the broad national interest, then it surely follows that senators would be expected to vote according only to the interest of their *own* province or region. Policies unpopular only in a given part of Canada would still likely become law, since any one region could be outvoted by the other regions combined. The only way that could be avoided would be if the reformed Senate developed a system of reciprocal deals whereby whatever was strongly opposed by *any* province or region would be blocked by *all* senators. In that case, the Senate would become a House of Obstruction, potentially thwarting more government initiatives than it approved.

Obstruction of one kind or another is, in fact, a real danger if we create a Senate that has both great power and a fresh constitutional mandate to use it. The existing Senate has from its beginning had the power to reject outright most legislation passed by the House of Commons. But because the Senate is an appointed body, senators have in recent times felt that they lack the moral right — except in the most extraordinary circumstances — to overrule the will of elected Members of Parliament. If the Senate is reformed, senators will understandably feel entitled to use whatever powers they are given under those reforms.

If those powers include the ability to block outright any legislation passed by the House of Commons, our national system of government will be thrown out of balance. It is in the nature of our parliamentary system that the prime minister and the cabinet are responsible to the House of Commons. If any government is no longer able to command a majority of votes in the House, that government falls. But what happens to this system if major government policies duly passed by the House start being regularly and permanently blocked by the Senate? Who will be accountable to Canadians for the consequences of legislative inaction resulting from a stalemate? How can the government be responsible for the state of the nation if it is not free to govern?

Canada already has enough powerful layers of political process to make the country difficult to govern as things stand. National leadership must already take into account the roles of provincial legislatures and provincial premiers, First Ministers' conferences which have become another level of government, and the House of Commons. Add to this a reformed Senate with a fresh mandate to overrule the Commons, and we might end up not with progress but with paralysis.

If the Senate is to be reformed, the key is not to get bogged down with an inflexible interpretation of slogans like "Triple-E" but to focus on what can realistically be done to give people a greater sense of fairness and balance. All the Es are in fact attainable, provided they are defined in a spirit of practicality. Senators can be "elected," if Canadians feel that is preferable to appointment. Representation can be "equal" — in the sense of *regional* equality. Quebec and Ontario would never agree to having the same number of senators as a tiny province like Prince Edward Island. But there could be, for instance, an equal number of senators from each of Atlantic Canada, Quebec, Ontario and the West. And the Senate could be "effective" without being made all-powerful. This could be done by providing it with a three-month suspensive veto, whereby any legislation not approved by the Senate within three months would still become law if it were re-passed by the House of Commons.

A Senate reformed along such lines could have the democratic legitimacy, the regional representation and the necessary power to serve as an effective chamber of sober second thought. If a government sought to ram through legislation that was strongly opposed in a particular region or was potentially damaging to the country as a whole, the Senate would be able to hold it up long enough for critics to take their case to the public and rally support. No government would be able to use its majority to push contentious policies into law before the country had a chance to realize what was happening.

Senate reform will never be the perfect remedy for regional grievances that some of its advocates are unrealistically leading people to expect. What reform of the Senate can do is update the institution and strengthen its ability to serve as one of the mechanisms through which the people of Canada can express their common will.

We cannot look to constitutional change to solve every problem in our country. The role of the Constitution is merely to provide the framework within which we can evolve and progress, while affirming the basic realities of our identity and common purpose. When one looks beyond the self-serving agendas of many politicians, the Canadian people are remarkably united in how they see those realities. This needless constitutional trauma to which we have been subjected, divisive and dangerous as it is, has taught us one important lesson. It has shown us how very precious and fragile our Canada is, how important we are to one another and how easily the balancing act that holds together a country as diverse as ours can be knocked askew if we stray too far from the "Canadian way." The Canadian people know that the real path to strengthening our country lies in our hearts and minds — in rediscovering our Canadian values and our shared commitment to work together toward fair participation and fair treatment for every individual and every region.

SIXTEEN

Where There's a Will

WE CANADIANS ARE ACCUSTOMED to challenges. We have never been afraid of the future nor doubtful of our ability as a nation to accomplish even the seemingly impossible. Previous generations created a cohesive nation out of vast wilderness, succeeded for a century and a quarter in maintaining the independence of that nation in the shadow of a giant and powerful neighbour and bequeathed to us a standard of living and a quality of life that today are the envy of much of the world. Today we, in our turn, have a new challenge to overcome, perhaps the most important one of all — the challenge of ensuring that a single episode of devastatingly damaging government is not allowed to destroy our spirit and permanently deflect us from our sense of who and what we are as a nation. The very survival of Canada depends on it.

We are in a state of crisis in the truest sense of the word: a turning point for better or worse. The Conservatives have set us on a course that is as un-Canadian as it is self-destructive. The comparatively brief period of dismantlement we have experienced under the current Tories has already left Canadians understandably demoralized, confused and despairing of the future. To continue to give up our values, our institutions and our uniquely Canadian approach to economic development and social justice ultimately can only mean giving up the existence of our nation. But there is still an alternative direction available to us. If we can return to the course that has served us so well throughout our history, all the immediate imperatives we face — restoring national unity, reviving our economy and regaining our country's independence — have solutions that are within reach. Our longer-term opportunities are without limit. Returning to this course requires us to rediscover precisely what the Tories have been most adept at taking away from us: our shared national will and sense of purpose.

We need to remember what our predecessors knew so well. It never occurred to them to question whether Canada was worth building or preserving, or whether they had the capacity to surmount obstacles. With quiet confidence, step by incremental step, generations of Canadians have overcome all their considerable challenges because they have had the unflagging *will* to prevail. Canada has, indeed, been built on layer upon layer of acts of national will, the sustained and determined collective will of the Canadian people.

The 14th-century Arabic historian Ibn Khaldun wrote of a quality he called "asabya," a cohesiveness that led the members of a society to be dedicated not only to their individual interests but to the well-being of one another. Societies with a high degree of "asabya" withstood wars, plagues, famines and every other manner of disaster and continued to thrive, while those that lacked this quality withered even in the absence of external threat. The Canadian experience, centuries later, bears out the validity of this concept. Our predecessors had "asabya" in abundance; that same quality is what we must find again within ourselves to begin our national recovery and move into the future with renewed confidence.

We need to remember afresh what it is to be Canadian. That we have succeeded in developing a unique society that has struck a delicate balance between the French and the English fact, between individual initiative and shared responsibility and between a strong central government and regional diversity is not because we are Canadian. Rather, we became Canadian in the process of meeting these challenges. The pursuit of balance and fairness, in a spirit of tolerance and sharing, has been the core of our national identity and the source of our cohesiveness. Now, more than any time in our history, we need a national government that adheres to these values.

We cannot give ourselves such a government by turning our backs in disgust on government itself. However much Canadians feel disillusioned with mainstream politicians, neither tuning out the political process nor voting for simplistic splinter parties can improve our situation. If we fail to take an interest in politics, the penalty we will pay is to be governed by people inferior to ourselves. And if we operate from the premise that everyone in politics is by definition self-serving and corrupt, we will ensure that only self-serving and corrupt people are willing to go into politics.

The political process functions best when people of proven quality and accomplishment are encouraged to run for Parliament. What has made it possible in the past to attract such people to politics in this country was a willingness among Canadians to presume that these men and women were seeking to make a positive contribution to our national life and to accord them a measure of respect. In recent years, however, cynicism has become rampant to the point where all participants in public life tend automatically to be regarded as vermin. This reaction to what we have been undergoing may be understandable, but it is profoundly self-defeating. The more this view persists, the more reluctant people who are already successful and respected in some other field will be to leave it in favour of subjecting themselves to scorn as politicians.

Instead we need to begin reversing the deterioration of our public life by renewing our commitment to the political process. This is a crucial time to reach out to the best people in our communities across the country — the men and women who most closely share our vision of how Canada should function — and vigorously encourage them to seek election. That is the most promising way for Canadians to reassert control over the governance of our nation.

We are currently in the hands of a government that, already at depths of unpopularity never before plumbed in our history, has chosen to function with total indifference to the wishes of ordinary Canadians and thus has placed itself beyond the reach of public opinion until the next election. But we must demand of our next government a return to the fundamental Canadian values on which our nation has been based. With these values as our guide, none of the damage that has been inflicted on Canada is irreversible.

We can restore national unity with a constitutional renewal that meets the real needs of the people of Quebec and of the other regions, that brings justice to the aboriginal people and that puts the ultimate power of decision over our Constitution in the hands of ordinary Canadians. Our economy can be resuscitated by a new mix of policies that ends our needless current hardship and gives us the tools to compete globally from a position of strength and confidence. We can reclaim our sovereignty by abrogating the free trade deal with the U.S. and diversifying our trade relationships to take advantage of opportunities in the Pacific Rim, newly industrializing countries and the emerging new Europe. Our social safety net and our cultural and transportation links can be repaired, strengthened and adapted to meet our changing needs for the 21st century.

With renewed independence and faith in ourselves, we can again be a positive force in the world in areas that have always been our strengths. We can, for instance, provide leadership on the environment. Beyond cleaning up our own air, land and waters, we can and should become a strong voice for global environmental responsibility. At a time when the greenhouse effect threatens to change the climate of our entire planet and we are told our children can no longer safely play outdoors because of holes in the ozone layer, it is inescapably clear that environmental degradation knows no national boundaries. Canada, as one of the first nations to have become active on environmental issues, is naturally positioned to take the lead in pushing for action worldwide. And we can also become major innovators in our own right. Why couldn't Canada, for example, be the nation to revolutionize transportation by developing a truly effective electric car to replace the polluting and resource-consuming vehicles used around the world today? The list of innovative environmental technologies we could pioneer is, in fact, virtually endless — developing new methods to clean up oil spills, to harness wind and solar energy, to dispose of toxic and other wastes and to harvest natural resources in environmentally sustainable ways.

Canada has also long been known and respected as a voice for decency and sanity in international politics. From our leadership in resolving the Suez crisis, through our government's opposition to the Vietnam war, to paving the way for a thawing of the Cold War and recognition of China, Canada has been able to exert an important and positive influence on world affairs. That influence is much needed today as global politics are being reshaped by developments in Eastern Europe.

Now that the countries of the former Soviet Union have embraced democracy as the West has been urging for half a century, the fate of the world may well depend on the quality of the Western response. If the United States and other countries including Canada continue to watch from the sidelines while starving, angry and desperate people in Russia and former Soviet bloc countries plead vainly for adequate help, we will never be forgiven by them. Unless there is massive aid and support from the West, economic and social collapse may well bring new hard-line regimes to power — and disillusioned populations will have good cause to agree that we truly are the enemy. At best, the resulting renewal of tensions will force us to re-arm, spending at least as much then on preparing for war as we might spend now on building a lasting peace. Canada alone cannot financially rescue Eastern Europe, of course. But on this, as on other issues in the past, we can hope to transform the course of events by combining our own example of aid with energetic advocacy and diplomacy on the world stage.

All this, and more, is possible for Canada. There are no limits to what we can accomplish. We do not have to settle into the despondency and decline into which our years of Conservative government have plunged us. If we can summon up again the will to be Canadian, that great shared collective will that created and shaped our country from its first days, there is still an alternative.

That alternative is to regain the path from which this government, an aberration in the historical direction of Canadian politics, has diverted us. It is to reject an imported ideology and hand-me-down economic policies borrowed from two former foreign leaders who are increasingly discredited in their own countries. It is to regain a healthy balance between federal and provincial governments, all working on our behalf in the best interest of the values that make us Canadian.

And it is, above all, to join together again in the great enterprise of nation-building that has been our strength throughout our history. It is by working together to build a positive vision of Canada's future that we can best rediscover our hope, our faith, our unity and our shared sense of purpose as a nation.